Believing - Salvation - Praise

*My Journey From Atheist to
Christian and Beyond*

by Bill Savage

Published by:

FriesenPress
Suite 300 – 852 Fort Street
Victoria, BC, Canada V8W 1H8

www.friesenpress.com

Distributed to the trade by The Ingram Book Company

Table of Contents

Dedication

It will become apparent during the reading of this book that my foremost dedication is to my Lord and Savior, Jesus Christ.

Secondly I dedicate it to my loving wife, Linda. She has taken care of me ever since I have known her, especially since 1999 with all the things she has gone through with me.

Third I wish to dedicate it to all those who have prayed for me, witnessed, taught and supported me all the years that I have known them. Many have gone on to be with the Lord, and I Praise his Holy Name for having placed them in my life.

Foreword

I caution anyone against taking scripture out of context. You should always study the word prayerfully with the Holy Spirit guiding you. I personally use the King James Version (KJV) and occasionally will cross reference it with other versions. I will also use commentaries, concordances, and other reference materials and books to obtain a clearer understanding.

In places where I am paraphrasing or only using part of a scripture, I have made a note, and you may look up, at the end of the book, the complete scriptures and verses either before or after which help to explain the scripture I am referencing. In addition on all endnotes I have included both the King James Version (KJV) and the New King James Version (NKJV).

I also caution anyone when using a different version to ensure that the meaning of the Scriptures has not been changed.

Jesus' words are in **bold print**.

Information for eBook users: - The endnote numbers are also hyperlinks to take you to the endnote reference and to return to the text. ( ) indicate the second reference to the same endnote.

Praise
Chapter 3(a)

No, it is not a publishing error; this is the start of chapter three. Think of it as a preface of sorts. The title of the book is *Believing – Salvation – Praise* which denotes the theme for the entire book and is a three word explanation for God's simple yet all inclusive plan for our lives. Early in my Christian life, approximately 30 years ago, I had an epiphany of God's plan for our lives. It is a complete circle, which involves our believing and trusting in him, his gracious salvation of our souls, and then our praise of him for what he has done. Through this praise others see Christ in us and want to know what it is that gives us the hope within us. Then through our obeying and his word others come to believe and the circle continues.

This presented a dilemma, in terms of how and where to start this book. Should I start with my believing or with the praise that he deserves for what he has done for me? Which chapter should be number one and which number three? I realized that my journey was similar to every other Christian in the world and that they would understand. Every Non-Christian has not reached the point of their soul's salvation and does not understand. What makes my story unique and worth reading? First I will state that I do not know the answer to that question; I just know that God told me to write it, and others encouraged me. I will go into detail about how this came about later.

Since January 17, 1999—through October 26, 2011—I have had at least seven heart attacks, six stents, quadruple bypass open heart surgery, two different types of cancer, seven different surgeries related to my cancers, two rounds of radiation treatments, and one chemotherapy treatment. So what? Thousands upon thousands of people—probably millions—have gone through way more. I am no one special; and everyone has loads of problems they are dealing with every day. As I finished writing and was ready to start contacting publishers, I printed copies and sent them to six preachers, six family members, and one close friend to ensure accuracy and receive their honest critique. I still could not believe that God wanted me—of all people—to write a book. One of my brother-in-laws asked me a simple question, and it turned out to be one of the first questions the publishers ask. Who was my targeted market? My reply was simple, "I have no idea! God told me to write it, so I did. I would hope that it might be encouraging to Christians, and more importantly, that it might help someone who does not know Christ as their personal Lord and Savior to come to accept him."

This may seem out of context, but I believe our country to be the greatest country on earth, and this is no accident. It was founded on the desire to be able to worship and on the belief that *In God We Trust*. The second line of our Declaration of Independence reads as follows, "We hold these truths to be self-evident, that all men are created equal, that they are endowed by their Creator with certain unalienable Rights, that among these are Life, Liberty and the pursuit of Happiness."

Our founding fathers held it to be a self-evident truth that all men are created equal. I am no better or any worse than any other person created. They also believed in a creator that gave us rights that were absolute, which included life, liberty and the pursuit of happiness. As you observe all peoples, all over the earth, they are no different than you and me. They are all seeking something, which they may not express in the same way, but are all pursuing their happiness. They may believe that financial security or political achievements will give them true happiness. They may believe that love, companionship, and family will achieve it for them.

There are countless stories of celebrities who have obtained wealth and then either overdosed on drugs, or got into trouble with the law and so on because they still had not found happiness and were still seeking that *something* which made them happy for longer than just a season. There are marriages that start out with a never-ending love only to dissolve a few years later because they didn't provide the expected happiness. Jobs which at first seem ideal, promising to provide for all needs, later disappear or turn out to be not as satisfying as they first appeared.

I have found, over the years, that the missing piece in people's lives, which they are so desperately seeking, is a true restoration and relationship with God. When we come to know God and pursue God's will in our lives, we automatically find the happiness, peace of mind, and love we have been seeking. It is my prayer that, if you are a Christian, this book and my testimony may uplift you and gives you encouragement in whatever circumstances you may be facing or that may lie ahead and place in your heart a desire to praise God in all things. It is furthermore my prayer that, if you do not know Christ, that through my praise and other true Christians you have met it may help you to understand that what you have been so desperately seeking in your life is at your very grasp and is yours freely for the asking.

I realize that at the time the disciple wrote the book of John that there were no printing presses, not to mention any digital publishing etc., but the last verse of the book of John is as follows:

"And there are also many other things which Jesus did, the which, if they should be written every one, I suppose that even the world itself could not contain the books that should be written. Amen" (John 21:25 KJV).

If I were able to recount only the blessings that God has shown to me, not counting the times he was looking after me and I was unaware, I cannot imagine how many books it would fill.

Let me make it clear that nothing said in this book is in any way boasting or bragging or lifting up myself but is only said to give God the Praise and to uplift his kingdom and bestow honor on his Son. **"That all *men* should honour the Son, even as they honour the Father. He that honoureth not the Son honoureth not the Father which hath sent him"** (John 5:23 KJV).

Again, my prayer is that, if only a portion of my testimony and Praise will help you in your walk with Christ, others may see the Light of God in you or help you to understand that God's Fellowship and Love is at your fingertips for the asking and that God will have thus accomplished his desire for my Life.

When first Saved I needed God's help in resolving several issues. The first I am going to group all together; they are the same worries or concerns that almost everyone has—making a living, food, shelter, clothing, etc. The second was tithing. The third was drinking and drugs, and the fourth was one that I didn't recognize at the time as being something that I needed God's help with. I will explain each in turn in part (b) of Chapter 3. But before I could rightly give God the praise for all the things he has done for me, I had to believe and come to know him personally.

Believing and trusting in him was the most difficult thing I have ever done in my life. Even after my salvation, there were times when instead of waiting on his answer to my prayers I would want to help him along. If I went ahead, it invariably went wrong, and he would have to then straighten things out for me as most any loving Father does. My son and daughter when they were both much younger came home on occasion and said Pop or Dad, I have messed things up and can I come home or can you please help me. Without question, but with a few stipulations, I did everything within my power to help them.

Lately with the shape our country has gotten into I have seen a Bible verse quoted more often than ever before: "If my people, which are called by my name, shall humble themselves, and pray, and seek my face, and turn from their wicked ways; then will I hear from heaven, and will forgive their sin, and will heal their land" (2 Chron. 7:14 KJV). God placed three or four stipulations on welcoming us home. I recently received an email requesting that I pray for our country, quoting this scripture. I tried to lovingly point out these three or four simple—but necessary—stipulations God placed on us before he would hear. First we must humble ourselves, secondly we must pray seeking him, and then also turn from our wicked ways. We must do all, then will he hear! This is not a political book, and I am not going to go off on a political digression but our country seems to have lost its way. We were founded on a list of *freedoms of*, not *freedoms from*, and have come to let the desires of a few over rule the will of the people. The rights of the few or even just one vigorously need to be protected but not at the expense of the many. Enough said; no more political opinions.

Back to my giving God the praise. On those occasions when I did not have the patience to wait on God; I praise him that he did have the loving patience to wait on me. In every case it would have only required my having enough faith and belief, and things would have worked out a whole lot sooner and better for me.

Therefore I will now start with Chapter 1 *Believing* and continue with my *Praise* Chapter in its rightful place after *Salvation*.

Believing
Chapter 1

Let your mind wander, imagining it is a cool crisp morning in early spring. Two young boys are walking to their little one room schoolhouse somewhere along the eastern coast of North Carolina. The year is 1904, and as they walk round a bend in the dirt road a horseless carriage comes round the corner almost running them over. After gaining their composure from jumping in the ditch, they continue their walk. Ahead of them, just above the treetops, is a full bright moon and the sun is just coming up to their backs.

Peter, matter-of-factly and apropos of nothing, states, "Someday man is going to fly to the moon!"

Tommy's immediate response is skeptical. "Ain't neither. You're nuts." And the conversation continues along these lines.

PETER: Will too, didn't you hear Mrs. Jones say yesterday in class what those Wright Brothers did at Kittyhawk.

TOMMY: You mean 'bout that *airplane*.

PETER: Yea!

TOMMY: I wanna see them fly that thing to the moon.

PETER: Don't be stupid. They ain't gonna fly that contraption to the moon, but someday they'll build one that can fly to the moon.

And the conversation goes back and forth till they reach the little school, and as they enter, Peter runs up to Mrs. Jones and looks back at his friend. "Mrs. Jones, tell him we will someday fly to the moon."

MRS. JONES: I don't know 'bout that Peter.

PETER: Yea but you said them brothers flew—

MRS. JONES: Flying a new confangled airplane is a long ways from flying to the moon.

PETER: But Mrs. Jones just think—

MRS. JONES: Enough of this foolishness. Both of you take your seats.

TOMMY: Ha! Ha! I told you!

PETER: Oh shut up, you'll see.

The subject was never mentioned again between them, but Peter always knew in his heart the eventual outcome.

Skip ahead to the year 1968 and Apollo 8 successfully completed its mission, orbiting the moon and returning home safely. Peter and Tommy are both watching the coverage on television and thinking of each other. Wondering what the other is doing since they had lost touch many years before. The difference is Peter is wondering why there is not some way, in this modern age of 1968, with all man has accomplished, that he and Tommy could not stay in touch and easily find each other. He does not know how—maybe via some sort of electronic *something* (they would one day call it the Internet).

The years have gone by, and both Peter and Tommy have since passed on, never getting to reunite with each other. Peter never getting to say *I told you so,* and Tommy never getting to acknowledge his friend had a far greater visionary mind than his own. By now you get the picture I am trying to paint. Peter had no problem believing in the yet unknown. I guess with that statement you are now thinking

'I know where this is heading,' but I challenge you to keep an open mind—like Peter—and keep reading.

I heard or read the following statement sometime ago, and it has stuck with me through the years. On many occasions it has guided my thought process. "We are all the total sum of our past experiences." Stop and think about that. Everything which has happened to us, everything we have read, everything that has been said to us, everything that we have been taught in schools or classes has affected what we are at this very moment.

Now I am going to ask you to put your imagination back to work. The year is approximately 1400 AD, and you are very fortunate to have been born into an affluent family. You are in class in what would be today's equivalent of one of the best colleges anywhere in the world, being taught by the leading scholars of that day. The subject class is astronomy with the professor leading the discussion of the different star formations.

It is being explained—and *proved* no less—that the stars rotate around the earth, coming back into position every so often. This is known because our earth is flat. So on and so on goes the education. Do you question it? Are you the total sum of your past experiences? Do you accept it as fact because some of the best minds know it to be true? If you are like most of us Tommies in the world, you go on studying; believing in what is comfortable and easy to believe. You also reject those things which are just too far out to comprehend. It is safe—or so you believe—to accept what you have been taught or experienced as the truth, and that is that.

I challenge you to stop and think about what *belief* or believing really is. I accept it as a state of mind. My copy of the Webster's Dictionary (Webster's Encyclopedia Of Dictionaries, New American Edition by Ottenheimer Publishers, Inc. Copyright 1958 by the Literary Press) defines it as follows:

be·lieve (bi · lēv') *v.t.* to regard as true; to trust; *v.i.* to have faith (in); to think; to suppose.

belief *n.* that which is believed; full acceptance of a thing as true; faith; a firm persuasion of the truth of a body of religious tenets.

believable *a.* credible.

In Peter's mind he had no problem accepting things unseen or yet unknown as facts that would take place. Tommy on the other hand only believed something when he could see, hear, touch, smell or taste it. In other words, if his five senses told him it was a fact, he could accept it, thus believing it. Again I am going to quote something I heard or read at some point in my life. "Most everyone can see apples on a tree, but only a rare individual can look at an apple and see trees."

If when you were at a certain age someone you loved and trusted told you not to touch the front of an oven because it was hot and would burn you. You would react in one of three ways. 1) You would trust and believe and not touch the oven. 2) You would touch it in spite of what was said to find out for yourself. 3) You would remain unsure but not touch it just in case they were right. You are the total sum of your past experiences at each point in your life. Genetic makeup affects each of us in how we come to those different stages and how we let each experience affect us, but with each of our individual genetic makeups and each of our own set of experiences it makes us who we are.

Once an individual who had been hired as a consultant to train myself and another employee in a new job was making a point that, when you are learning something completely new, you take small steps and break it down into smaller components and learn each of those and then put it all together. He knew I loved to snow ski and so, to illustrate his point, he used the following example. His statement was that, when I was learning to snow ski, I did not start off on the first day by going to the top of the mountain. I began on the bunny or beginner's slope, and as I learned and gained experience I would go up the chair lift. I busted out laughing out loud. I had to explain that I understood and could comprehend the example he was making but something in my past experiences had made me a little nuts to say the very least. On my first day I did exactly that. I went to the top of the mountain. I learned it was a mistake, and I would not dare train anyone else to ski by doing that. But nonetheless it was where I was during that part of my life. I make this point because I was always the type to believe I could do anything and had faith, which is to say *the substance of things hoped for, the evidence of things not seen* (Heb. 11:1 KJV), in my own abilities to carry me through whatever I encountered in life.

On to believing—do you believe the following?

(Remember, are you going to believe for the rest of your life that the world is flat?)

Many billions of years ago there was some sort of big bang or explosion. All the masses of elements and gases started rapidly moving or flying away from the point of the explosion. As they traveled through the vast nothingness of space, they began to collect together just by chance. Some of the gases collecting together forming stars and the elements or masses coming together were forming planets. The stars having different degrees of density and over the billions of years some would expand, exploding again while others would collapse in on themselves etc. and so on. As the planets formed they would eventually cool. With the elements being just right water would form and light from the stars would cause photosynthesis and an amoeba or single cell life form would then magically appear. From that amoeba, two or three would then, through evolution, join together forming new and different life forms. Again over billions of years these few cells would evolve into fish, dinosaurs and man. Forget what you have heard about Darwin's theory that man and ape came from the same ancestors. We all came from fish and going on back we all came from single cell amoebas. This is paraphrased a great deal and shortened tremendously, but in a nutshell it is the essence of the theory of evolution. Do your senses tell you this is hard or easy to believe? It is pretty far-fetched and way out there, but it is exactly what I thought and believed for many a year. It is what I was taught in school, and I accepted it as fact, and it became what I believed. At one point in my life when I was seventeen, I had tried accepting God but dismissed him within a couple of weeks as not real. If God was not real, what was left but evolution? Some scientists have now come to the conclusion that some of the laws of physics do not work well together. The only way they can be explained is through some new theory called the string theory. In addition they have recently found life forms at the bottom of the oceans that do not require photosynthesis too exist. Remember that at one point the best minds in the world knew beyond a reasonable doubt that the world was flat.

When I was twenty-nine, the events which had made me the total sum of my past experiences prompted me to question what I believed and had faith in. What was life all about? Was it just an endless nothing? I believed people who had Faith in God were just weak, looking for something else to be in control so that they had an excuse for everything that happened to them. I could go to the top of the mountain my first day skiing. If circumstances had been a little different I could have been President of the United States. I was in charge of most of the things that happened, and the ones that I could not control, I could deal with. After all everything in life was just a chance anyway, even all the way back to the big bang. But if everything was just a chance, then I was not really in control. Again what was the purpose of life—with all of its good times, not to mention its headaches and problems? Sound like rambling and a vicious circle? Looking back at that point in my life, I realize that it was. I now know—not only believe—what is real. Forgive me, for I am jumping ahead of myself. I will come back to that later.

In life we constantly have choices to make, and most of the time we have several options, which guide our choices. For an example let us take the automobile. In what man calls today's civilized world it has almost become a necessity. If it breaks down, we have several choices.

1. We can say we just do not have the money to get it fixed or buy another one and that we are going to get by without one until we can afford to do something. This brings about several other choices or possibilities. We are going to walk where we need to go. We will have our friends pick us up to get back and forth to work. Family can take us to the store, etc. We will use public transportation to get around if it is available or we can afford a bicycle or motor bike if we live in a climate where that is an option.

2. We will have the car repaired even if it takes getting a rebuilt engine or something.

3. We will buy a used car in a price range that we can afford.

4. We will go ahead and buy that new car we have been wanting anyway.

Rather than trying to list all the possibilities I am sure you see that with each of the options two, three and four they leave open several other obvious choices. Such as who is going to fix it, what price range can we afford, what make and model and so on.

The point I am trying to make is that you have a choice in what you BELIEVE. It may come from the total sum of your past experiences, but you have a CHOICE. Through the process of elimination, you normally narrow it down to one or two best choices by deductive reasoning.

Do you honestly believe, in your mind and heart, that you accidentally came from an amoeba or single cell and have evolved into what you are today? Do you honestly believe, in your mind and heart, that it all started from a massive big bang? I did.

All the people in the world BELIEVE one of three things.

1. the theory of evolution

2. that a supernatural power created

3. they have not forced themselves to face which of the above two they believe. They will say they do not know or they have not given it much thought.

If you honestly believe that we are all an accident and there is absolutely no possibility of changing your mind, then you may as well stop reading. I thank you for your time and only ask that you pass this book on to a friend or a loved one that you care about. If there is a question or doubt like I began to have at twenty-nine, maybe you have believed that the world is flat because it is what all the great minds of the day have been saying, then please continue.

If it is not a big accident then what else is left, other than someone created it? If someone created it, who is or was it? The theory of *intelligent design* perhaps? How can you believe that some intelligent designer or creator caused what happened any more than you can believe that it all started by accident? Examine the options through deductive reasoning. That is right, the same process you used in making the decision as what to do about that broken down old car, although this decision is a lot more vital to you than a mere automobile. For the sake of discussion at this point I am going to call the one who created it God—the intelligent designer.

As a young boy of eleven, I was out playing in the woods around the house of a relative I seldom visited. I did not know my way around. All of a sudden I realized I had no idea where I was or how to get back to their house. Even at eleven I was pretty calm and figured I would find my way back. All I had to do was too keep walking, and I would come out on a road and someone could lead me home. That worked for quite awhile, but I eventually began to get concerned because I was realizing I was really lost and the road home was not as easy to find as I had thought it would be. Finally I heard someone calling me and headed straight to their voices. Mom and Dad were worried; of course, I played it cool and acted like I did not understand what the big deal was. If you are not sure of what your beliefs are and the path to find your way home is not that easy to find or is not clear, please keep reading.

First, about God! I have heard Believing in God is compared to going to town. There is more than one road that leads to town, more than one way to get there. These people are in a sense trying to use a parable to compare earthly things or physical things to spiritual understanding. In order for it to be a *true* spiritual parable or comparison, it has to be true in a physical sense and also true in terms of spiritual meaning. There is a broad and a narrow way[1]. They may both lead to town but they do not both lead to God. There are plenty of religions in the world and plenty of different beliefs. In my copy of the Webster's Dictionary it defines *religion* as: *n, belief in supernatural power which governs universe; recognition of God as object of worship; practical piety; any system of faith and worship.*

If you do not believe you came from an accident and you believe that some supernatural power (God) governs the universe, you have a system of faith and worship or a form of religion.

Let us examine some of those religions. It will probably become apparent very quickly where I am headed, but keep the deductive reasoning working. You are trying to make a decision as to what you believe, what you are going to put your faith in, whether the world is flat or not, whether man will ever fly not only to the moon but to *Mars*.

Please understand I am not trying to put down any religion, and I am not singling out any particular groups or religions. I am not a scholar nor am I a theologian, but I am trying to help you understand *my* deductive reasoning, which has brought me to the point of where I am today. If the following statement applies to anyone, please keep reading; it will later become clear—**because of the word, by and by he is offended.**[2] For the time being let us say that some of the below listed may have been prophets, men of God, etc. That is not the point I am trying to get across.

The following six examples are taken in part directly from my World Book Encyclopedia, (© 1980, USA by World Book-Childcraft International, Inc.)

1. Baal; BAY ul, was the name of an ancient god worshiped by the Hebrews. The word means lord, or master. The Hebrews borrowed the worship of Baal from the Canaanites (see Canaanites) because Baal was the god of all growth; his worship was connected with the tilling of the soil. Tyre, Sidom, Lebanon, and other places each had its own Baal.

2. Greek Gods. The Greeks worshiped many gods. Most Greeks believed their gods were superhuman beings that were friendly to mankind. They felt that men could anger the gods only by impiety or insolence. The Greeks did not live in terror of their gods, as other ancient peoples did. Each city-state had its own minor gods and worshiped them in its own way. The Greeks regarded Homer and Hesiod as great teachers, and generally accepted the gods these poets described as the most important. Zeus, who lived on Mount Olympus, was the chief god, ruling men and the other gods. The other important gods were all related to Zeus. Apollo was god of light, music, and youth; Dionysus of wine;

   And it goes on but you get the picture. Paul said, "*Ye men of Athens, I perceive that in all things ye are too superstitious. For as I passed by, and beheld your devotions, I found an altar with this inscription, TO THE UNKNOWN GOD. Whom therefore ye ignorantly worship...*"[3]

3. Buddha (Around 575–475 BC) Buddha is the title given to the founder of Buddhism. His name was Siddhartha Gautama. The title Buddha means enlightened one. At around 80 years old he took ill and died having his body burned and his bones distributed as sacred relics.

4. Muhammad (Around 570–632 AD) His life and teachings form the basis of the Islamic Religion. He is said

to be the last messenger of God. He completed the scared teachings of such earlier prophets as Abraham, Moses and Jesus. Muslims respect him but do not worship him. Muhammad died in 632 AD and his tomb is in the Prophet's Mosque in Medina.

5. John Wesley (1703–1791 AD) A founder of Methodism. John Wesley was a clergyman of the Church of England.

6. Joseph Smith (1805–1844 AD) Founder of the Mormon Church officially Church of Jesus Christ of Latter-day Saints. Smith is said to have been a prophet from God and the Mormons claim that the Church as established by Christ did not survive. God and Jesus Christ appeared to Smith and told him not to join any existing Churches and sent an angel giving him gold tablets, which he translated into the Book of Mormons.

As I stated earlier, I did not list these examples to offend anyone, and I do not claim to be a religious expert. The only reason for picking the ones I did is because they are some of the better known that came to mind. The reason for listing any is to make a point that you are trying to determine in what you are to believe. If you are not going to believe that you are an accident here only by evolution, then who and what can you believe in?

When evaluating my beliefs, I started to realize that of all the religious beliefs and leaders only one was supposedly alive, and that was Jesus. After more detailed study, to the best of my knowledge, I realized that no other founders of various religions have had the claims made about them that Jesus has.

Consider the following statements. The family he would be born into, the place of his birth, and that a forerunner would announce his ministry. Details of how he would die and who he would die with, where he would be buried, and that he would be raised from the dead were all foretold long before any of them would come about.

I once read a Sunday School lesson where the writer made a very valid point. I may not quote it exactly but it was along the following lines. Many have said that Jesus was a great teacher and/or prophet but not the Messiah or Savior of the world. If you study the words of Jesus this cannot be true. He has to be what he claims or he is one of the biggest liars and cruelest persons that have ever lived. Jesus said, **"I am the way, the truth, and the life: no man cometh unto the Father, but by me."** (John 14:6 KJV) If this is true then he is the only way to God. As we go deeper into what the Bible says about Jesus and his own words as recorded by different authors. It will become apparent that it either has to be true or he has misled millions and millions of people. Remember the earlier quote (there is a broad and a narrow way [1]) in reference to the fact that there is more than one way to town or God. Jesus said **"Enter ye in at the strait gate: for wide *is* the gate, and broad *is* the way, that leadeth to destruction, and many there be which go in thereat: Because strait *is* the gate, and narrow *is* the way, which leadeth unto life, and few there be that find it."** (Matt. 7:13-14 KJV)

Before getting into some of the actual predictions or prophecies about Jesus and his teachings, I have one more thing for you to consider. Imagine that tomorrow a huge asteroid (one of those big rocks accidentally formed in space from the big bang) hits earth with such force that life as we know it would be changed forever. The world might, after that, start referring to time as before the event (or asteroid) and after the event.

Some religions have their own calendars, but the general population of the whole world started telling time by before Christ's birth and after his birth. The difference one man made changed the way the whole world told time. It had never happened before and has not happened since. BC stands for Before Christ and AD stands for anno Domini (in the year of Our Lord). I personally like to think of them as BC (Before Christ) and AD (After Deliverance)

You may be asking, *Deliverance from what?* Remember, you are trying to find your way to what you believe and what you are going to place your faith in. Deductive reasoning on many things can give you several options and help you to narrow down your choices but on some things there are only two choices. For example; you are either dead or alive, you are either swimming or you are not, and according to Jesus' teachings you are either saved or you are lost. When I was out in the woods I either knew where I was or I was LOST, regardless of how I tried to fool myself. Mankind will try to apply its own beliefs or arguments to each of these, but they are wrong. "There is a way which seemeth right unto a man, but the end thereof *are* the ways of death." (Prov. 14:12 KJV)

Mankind will argue that before so many weeks an embryo is not really life or that when brain waves are no longer present or you cannot breathe on your own you are already dead. Mankind will argue that doing the dog paddle is a form of swimming; it is keeping your head above water. As I stated earlier in this chapter, mankind will argue there is more than one way to God; therefore, there is more than one way to Heaven or to be saved.

That analogy would be true if they changed only one part of their thinking. There is more than one way to come to the conclusion that Christ Jesus is the only way to God and therefore heaven. Again repeating myself from earlier— we are all the total sum of our past experiences. We may, through deductive reasoning and different experiences, come to the belief that Jesus is the way, the truth, and the life: and that no man cometh unto the Father, but by him. Regardless of how we reach that belief, if everything said about Jesus and everything he said is true, then it is the only true belief.

You may be saying to yourself, *I have read enough, and why should I believe?* I will go into that in more detail shortly, but first before anyone can be saved they have to realize they are lost. You are either one or the other. No maybe or no half way, it is either one or the other. If you do not know of the exact instance that you were saved then you are lost. Being saved is simple and easy, and I will explain in detail in Chapter 2, but again you have to accept the fact that you are either saved or you are lost. I am being almost redundant on this point, but sometimes people expect God to save them from hell and never accept the point that they are lost. I know I did it!

A lot of people want to believe that they are basically good people, and in a lot of cases that they have a big heart and help other people all the time, and therefore they hope they are going to heaven. A couple of scriptures and parables come to mind in addition to the ones mentioned above that no one can come to the Father other than by Jesus. "All our righteousnesses *are* as filthy rags"[4] and "For by grace are ye saved through faith; and that not of yourselves; *it is* the gift of God: Not of works, lest any man should boast" (Eph. 2:8–9 KJV). Some want to use the scripture out of the bible that a corrupt tree cannot bring forth good fruit, but they forget or do not apply other scriptures in Jesus' own words such as, **"Abide in me, and I in you. As the branch cannot bear fruit of itself, except it abide in the vine; no more can ye, except ye abide in me. I am the vine, ye are the branches: He that abideth in me, and I in him, the same bringeth forth much fruit: for without me ye can do nothing"** (John 15:4–5 KJV) and another scripture, **"Not every one that saith unto me, Lord, Lord, shall enter into the kingdom of heaven; but he that doeth the will of my Father which is in heaven. Many will say to me in that day, Lord, Lord, have we not prophesied in thy name? and in thy name have cast out devils? and in thy name have done many wonderful works? And then will I profess unto them, I never knew you: depart from me, ye that work iniquity"** (Matt. 7:21–23 KJV).

In Jesus' own words, without him knowing us, our works are not considered wonderful even if we do them in his name. The Bible and Jesus himself make many claims. If they are true, we can count on life everlasting with him and God in Heaven. Again, I am getting ahead of myself and jumping to being saved ahead of believing.

According to the Bible and Jesus himself after he was put to death—crucified on the cross—he arose or was brought back to life after the third day. Prior to this many things had been foretold or prophesied about Jesus. You hear a lot today about Nostradamus in tabloids and game shows. He lived from 1503–1566 and was an astrologist and physician who wrote a book of prophecies but they are vague and open to interpretation. Of all the religious leaders, Jesus is the only one that his birth, death and resurrection were prophesied before it happened. He is the only one that claims to be alive today. In the news just recently astrology has been turned upside down. There are now thirteen signs instead of twelve and some people who believed they were under one sign and had certain influences now have different ones. (I guess they believed the world was flat and now have to believe something different.)

The Bible is a book containing various books and letters written over approximately 1500 years by approximately 40 different authors. Some containing history, some containing prophecies of events that at the time of their writing were in the future, but have since come true, and some containing prophecies of things which will still come to pass. Many people say the Bible is not or cannot be true. Over the generations things they say could not be true have been proven to actually have taken place. They then try to come up with other explanations. For hundreds of years mankind said the whole world could not have been completely flooded. Then archaeologist found what they believe to be Noah's Ark and they hurry to try and come up with other explanations such as the melting of the ice age or a local flood of the region which accounts for the story.

I heard a joke once about a story in the Bible that was cute and demonstrates the point that people either believe or they do not. The story in question is God parting the Red Sea for Moses and the children of Israel when he brought them out of Egypt and from under the bondage of the Pharaoh. It goes like this, a young boy was sitting and reading his Bible in a park and said out loud, 'Praise the Lord.' A man who was schooled and very knowledgeable in the bible was walking by, and he stopped and asked the young boy what he was praising God about. The boy replied, 'I was just reading the story of how God parted the Red Sea for Moses and saved them.' The man proceeded to explain to the boy that through study of the history and circumstances at the time this event took place that the Red Sea at that point was not but about ten inches deep and that a strong wind could have held the water back. The boy thanked the gentleman for explaining that to him and the man started on his way. Then he heard the boy say again, *'Praise the Lord,'* this time even louder. His curiosity got the best of him, and he went back and asked the boy what he was praising God about this time. The young boy said I was just reading where God drowned all those soldiers and horses with only ten inches of water.

We either believe or do not; we are either saved or lost. There are many scriptures that tell us the Bible is God's Word, but you have to believe the Bible before you can accept it as from God. To me I always felt that if I could understand the Bible then maybe I could believe it. Not until I believed it did I begin to understand it. Why should we believe? Starting with the items of prophecies I mentioned earlier about Jesus we will examine each one. There are many prophesies in the Bible which pertain to historical events which were prophesied many years before their taking place, but for this book I am only going to discuss some of the ones which pertain directly to Jesus.

Keep in mind that most of these books or references in the Bible were written by different authors, hundreds of years apart, all prophesying each point of Jesus' life.

SIX PROPHESIES CONCERNING JESUS.

One — The family he would be born into!

The Prophecy

> ✧ *And I will bless them that bless thee, and curse him that curseth thee: and in thee shall all families of the earth be blessed.* (Gen. 12:3 KJV) — God was telling Abraham to leave his country and go where he would show

him and all the families of the earth would be blessed through him.

❖ *And God said, Sarah thy wife shall bear thee a son indeed; and thou shalt call his name Isaac: and I will establish my covenant with him for an everlasting covenant, and with his seed after him.* (Gen. 17:19 KJV) — God telling Abraham he would have a son named Isaac and that Jesus would be his descendant.

❖ *And in thy seed shall all the nations of the earth be blessed; because thou hast obeyed my voice.* (Gen. 22:18 KJV) — This was telling Abraham that because of his obedience to God's command not just some but all the nations on earth were going to be blessed through a descendant of his.

❖ *I shall see him, but not now: I shall behold him, but not nigh: there shall come a Star out of Jacob and a Scepter shall rise out of Israel, and shall smite the corners of Moab, and destroy all the children of Sheth.* (Num. 24:17 KJV) — Jesus would be of Jacob's seed.

❖ *Of the increase of his government and peace there shall be no end, upon the throne of David, and upon his kingdom, to order it, and to establish it with judgment and with justice from henceforth even for ever. The zeal of the Lord of hosts will perform this.* (Isa. 9:7 KJV) — Jesus would be the heir to the throne of King David and rule with judgment and justice forever.

All the above prophesy about Jesus being the descendant of Abraham, Isaac, Jacob and King David and ruling for ever was written before his birth. The following was written after his birth.

The Fulfillment

❖ *He shall be great, and shall be called the Son of the Highest: and the Lord God shall give unto him the throne of his father David: And he shall reign over the house of Jacob for ever; and of his kingdom there shall be no end.* (Luke 1:32–33 KJV) — The angel Gabriel was telling Mary who her baby Jesus would be.

✧ *The book of the generation of Jesus Christ, the son of David, the son of Abraham. Abraham begat Isaac; and Isaac begat Jacob; and Jacob begat Judas and his brethren; And Judas begat Phares and Zara of Thamar; and Phares begat Esrom; and Esrom begat Aram; And Aram begat Aminadab; and Aminadab begat Naasson; and Naasson begat Salmon; And Salmon begat Booz of Rachab; and Booz begat Obed of Ruth; and Obed begat Jesse; And Jesse begat David the king; and David the king begat Solomon of her that had been the wife of Urias; And Solomon begat Roboam; and Roboam begat Abia; and Abia begat Asa; And Asa begat Josaphat; and Josaphat begat Joram; and Joram begat Ozias; And Ozias begat Joatham; and Joatham begat Achaz; and Achaz begat Ezekias; And Ezekias begat Manasses; and Manasses begat Amon; and Amon begat Josias; And Josias begat Jechonias and his brethren, about the time they were carried away to Babylon: And after they were brought to Babylon, Jechonias begat Salathiel; and Salathiel begat Zorobabel; And Zorobabel begat Abiud; and Abiud begat Eliakim; and Eliakim begat Azor; And Azor begat Sadoc; and Sadoc begat Achim; and Achim begat Eliud; And Eliud begat Eleazar; and Eleazar begat Matthan; and Matthan begat Jacob; And Jacob begat Joseph the husband of Mary, of whom was born Jesus, who is called Christ. So all the generations from Abraham to David are fourteen generations; and from David until the carrying away into Babylon are fourteen generations; and from the carrying away into Babylon unto Christ are fourteen generations.* (Matt. 1:1–17 KJV)

The above written after Jesus' birth gives the generations fulfilling the prophecy that God would bless all the nations of the earth through Abraham's seed.

Two — The place of his birth!

The Prophecy

But thou, Bethlehem Ephratah, though thou be little among the thousands of Judah, yet out of thee shall he come forth unto me that is to be ruler in Israel; whose goings forth have been from of old, from everlasting. (Mic. 5:2 KJV) — Jesus who had been from old and was everlasting would come out of Bethlehem.

The Fulfillment

And Joseph also went up from Galiee, out of the city of Nazareth, into Judaea, unto the city of David, which is called Bethlehem; (because he was of the house and lineage of David:) To be taxed with Mary his espoused wife, being great with child. And so it was, that, while they were there, the days were accomplished that she should be delivered. And she brought forth her firstborn son, and wrapped him in swaddling clothes, and laid him in a manager; because there was no room for them in the inn. (Luke 2:4–7 KJV) — Even though Joseph and Mary lived in the city of Nazareth in Galiee circumstances were created at the time Jesus was to be born that they had to travel to Bethlehem where Jesus was born, fulfilling the prophecy that he would be born there.

Three — A forerunner would announce his ministry!

The Prophecy

 ❖ *The voice of him that crieth in the wilderness, Prepare ye the way of the LORD, make straight in the desert a highway for our God.* (Isa. 40:3 KJV)

 ❖ *Behold, I will send my messenger, and he shall prepare the way before me: and the Lord, whom ye seek, shall suddenly come to his temple, even the messenger of the covenant, whom ye delight in: behold he shall come, saith the Lord of hosts.* (Mal. 3:1 KJV) — The fact that John the Baptist would be a forerunner before Christ Jesus and prepare the way for him was prophesied before the birth of Jesus.

The following was also written of John the Baptist. Gabriel, an angel of the Lord, appeared to Zacharias the Husband of Elizabeth and the father of John the Baptist and told him the following pertaining to John:

> ✧ *And thou shalt have joy and gladness; and many shall rejoice at his birth. For he shall be great in the sight of the Lord, and shall drink neither wine nor strong drink; and he shall be filled with the Holy Ghost, even from his mother's womb. And many of the children of Israel shall he turn to the Lord their God. And he shall go before him in the spirit and power of Elias, to turn the hearts of the fathers to the children, and the disobedient to the wisdom of the just; to make ready a people prepared for the Lord.* (Luke 1:14–17 KJV)

The Fulfillment

In those days came John the Baptist, preaching in the wilderness of Judaea, And saying, Repent ye: for the kingdom of heaven is at hand. For this is he that was spoken of by the prophet Esaias, saying, The voice of one crying in the wilderness, Prepare ye the way of the Lord, make his path straight. And the same John had his raiment of camel's hair, and a leathern girdle about his loins; and his meat was locusts and wild honey. Then went out to him Jerusalem, and all Judaea, and all the region round about Jordan, And were baptized of him in Jordan, confessing their sins.

But when he saw many of the Pharisees and Sadducees come to his baptism, he said unto them, O generation of vipers, who hath warned you to flee from the wrath to come? Bring forth therefore fruits meet for repentance: And think not to say within yourselves, We have Abraham to our father: for I say unto you, that God is able of these stones to raise up children unto Abraham. And now also the axe is laid unto the root of the trees: therefore every tree which bringeth not forth good fruit is hewn down, and cast into the fire. I indeed baptize you with water unto repentance: but he that cometh after me is mightier than I, whose shoes I am not worthy to bear: he shall baptize you with the Holy Ghost, and with fire: Whose fan is in his hand, and he will throughly purge his floor, and gather his wheat into the garner; but he will burn up the chaff with unquenchable fire.

Then cometh Jesus from Galilee to Jordan unto John, to be baptized of him. But John forbad him, saying, I have need to be baptized of thee, and comest thou to me? And Jesus answering said unto him, **Suffer it to be so now: for thus it becometh us to fulfil all righteousness.** *Then he suffered him. And Jesus, when he was baptized, went up straightway out of the water: and, lo, the heavens were opened unto him, and he saw the Spirit of God descending like a dove, and lighting upon him: And lo a voice from heaven, saying, This is my beloved Son, in whom I am well pleased.* (Matt. 3:1–17 KJV)

Four — Details of how he would die and who he would die with!

The Prophecy

- ❖ *But he was wounded for our transgressions, he was bruised for our iniquities: the chastisement of our peace was upon him; and with his stripes we are healed.* (Isa. 53:5 KJV)

- ❖ *Therefore will I divide him a portion with the great, and he shall divide the spoil with the strong; because he hath poured out his soul unto death: and he was numbered with the transgressors; and he bare the sin of many, and made intercession for the transgressors.* (Isa. 53:12 KJV)

❖ *And I will pour upon the house of David, and upon the inhabitants of Jerusalem, the spirit of grace and of supplications: and they shall look upon me whom they have pierced, and they shall mourn for him, as one mourneth for his only son, and shall be in bitterness for him, as one that is in bitterness for his firstborn.* (Zech. 12:10 KJV)

❖ *All they that see me laugh me to scorn: they shoot out the lip, they shake the head, saying, He trusted on the LORD that he would deliver him: let him deliver him, seeing he delighted in him.* (Ps. 22:7–8 KJV)

❖ *I may tell all my bones: they look and stare upon me. They part my garments among them, and cast lots upon my vesture.* (Ps. 22:17–18 KJV)

❖ *He keepeth all his bones: not one of them is broken.* (Ps. 34:20 KJV)

❖ *They gave me also gall for my meat; and in my thirst they gave me vinegar to drink.* (Ps. 69:21 KJV)

The Fulfillment

❖ *For when we were yet without strength, in due time Christ died for the ungodly ... But God commendeth his love toward us, in that, while we were yet sinners, Christ died for us.* (Rom. 5:6, 8 KJV)

❖ *And with him they crucify two thieves; the one on his right hand, and the other on his left. And the scripture was fulfilled, which saith, and he was numbered with the transgressors.* (Mark 15:27–28 KJV)

❖ *They gave him vinegar to drink mingled with gall: and when he had tasted thereof, he would not drink. And they crucified him, and parted his garments, casting lots: that it might be fulfilled which was spoken by the prophet, they parted my garments among them, and upon my vesture did they cast lots.* (Matt. 27:34–35 KJV)

⬧ *Then came the soldiers, and brake the legs of the first, and of the other which was crucified with him. But when they came to Jesus, and saw that he was dead already, they brake not his legs; But one of the soldiers with a spear pierced his side, and forthwith came there out blood and water. And he that saw it bare record, and his record is true: and he knoweth that he saith true, that ye might believe. For these things were done, that the scripture should be fulfilled, a bone of him shall not be broken. And again another scripture saith, they shall look on him whom they pierced.* (John 19:32–36)

⬧ *And the people stood beholding. And the rulers also with them derided him, saying, He saved others; let him save himself, if he be Christ, the chosen of God.* (Luke 23:35 KJV)

⬧ *Then saith he to Thomas,* **Reach hither thy finger, and behold my hands; and reach hither thy hand, and thrust it into my side: and be not faithless, but believing.** (John 20:27 KJV)

Five — Where he would be buried!

The Prophecy

And he made his grave with the wicked, and with the rich in his death; because he had done no violence, neither was any deceit in his mouth. (Isa. 53:9 KJV)

The Fulfillment

When the even was come, there came a rich man of Arimathaea, named Joseph, who also himself was Jesus' disciple: He went to Pilate, and begged the body of Jesus. Then Pilate commanded the body to be delivered. And when Joseph had taken the body, he wrapped it in a clean linen cloth, And laid it in his own new tomb, which he had hewn out in the rock: and he rolled a great stone to the door of the sepulchre, and departed. (Matt. 27:57–60)

Six — That he would be raised from the dead!

The Prophecy

> ❖ *For thou wilt not leave my soul in hell; neither wilt thou suffer thine Holy One to see corruption.* (Ps. 16:10 KJV)

> ❖ *But God will redeem my soul from the power of the grave: for he shall receive me. Se'lah.* (Ps. 49:15 KJV)

The Fulfillment

And he saith unto them, Be not affrighted: Ye seek Jesus of Nazareth, which was crucified: he is risen; he is not here: behold the place where they laid him. But go your way, tell his disciples and Peter that he goeth before you into Galilee: there shall ye see him, as he said unto you. (Mark 16:6–7)

They are many, many more scriptures which give reference and validation to these prophecies and their fulfillment, but they are for your later study. The important thing I want to bring out at this time is that all of these are not only prophecies and their fulfillment about Jesus; but of, The Christ, The Messiah, The Savior, God's only begotten Son, The Lord, etc.

Jesus himself said, after he was raised from the dead and ate the fish and honeycomb, "… **These *are* the words which I spake unto you, while I was yet with you, that all things must be fullfilled, which were written in the law of Moses, and *in* the prophets, and *in* the Psalms, concerning me.** Then opened he their understanding, that they might understand the scriptures, And said unto them, **Thus it is written, and thus it behoved Christ to suffer, and to rise from the dead the third day: And that repentance and remission of sins should be preached in his name amoung all nations, beginning at Jerusalem. And ye are witnesses of these things.**" (Luke 24:44–48 KJV)[5]

Again, these prophesies were not only made of Jesus but they were made pertaining to

The Christ, The Messiah, The Savior, The only begotten son of God.

I could go on and on, but I just wanted to use enough scripture to show that every detail of Christ's life was foretold or prophesied before it took place. Keep in mind I am challenging your beliefs and trying to explain how I came to mine. At the very start I purposely used the names of Peter and Tommy in the fictitious story for a reason.

1st Apostle Peter told Jesus, "Thou art the Christ, the Son of the living God."[6] He Believed in things yet to come!

2nd Apostle Thomas believed not without being shown and said, "Except I shall see in his hands the print of the nails, and put my finger into the print of the nails, and thrust my hand into his side, I will not believe."[7]

Are *you* going to Believe or are *you* going to wait and see?

Remember I said I thought that if I could understand the Bible then maybe I could believe it. As Jesus himself opened the understanding of the apostles that they might understand the scriptures, once I Believed and got Saved, the Spirit started showing and explaining the scriptures to me in a way that made sense and I could understand—again I apologize, but I am jumping ahead and I will explain more about that later.

Back to the *big question!*

Did you come into existence by a big bang and the resulting evolution, or was the big bang caused by an intelligent designer, super being, spiritual entity, God. In the beginning God created the heaven and the earth. (Gen. 1:1 KJV and NKJV)

Before proceeding, one more question for you pertaining to space; have you ever asked yourself, where or what is at the end of space? At the outer edge of space, what is beyond— more space, it goes on forever. And if there is no end then there cannot be a center.

If you rule out the theory of evolution and say it just cannot be, it leaves too much to chance and haphazard circumstances, then what is left? An intelligent designer; God! If you decide through deductive reasoning to explore the possibility or option that there is an Intelligent Designer or a God, then you have to evaluate him relative to yourself. Remember, the total sum of your past experiences is what makes you who you are today. It is all you know, so that is where the comparison has to start. If he is able to speak into existence the heavens and the earth, *Who* or *What* does that make me and you in c*omparison* to *Him*?

Here I am going to quote several scriptures to get you to thinking.

⬧ The fool hath said in his heart, *There* is no God. (Ps. 14:1 KJV)

⬧ But, beloved, be not ignorant of this one thing, that one day *is* with the Lord as a thousand years, and a thousand years as one day. (2 Peter 3:8 KJV)

⬧ For all have sinned, and come short of the glory of God; (Rom. 3:23 KJV)

⬧ For the wages of sin *is* death; but the gift of God *is* eternal life through Jesus Christ our Lord. (Rom. 6:23 KJV)

⬧ But we are all as an unclean *thing*, and all our righteousnesses *are* as filthy rags ... (Isa. 64:6-8 KJV)[8]

⬧ In the beginning was the Word, and the Word was with God, and the Word was God. The same was in the beginning with God. All things were made by him; and without him was not any thing made that was made. In him was life; and the life was the light of men. And the light shineth in darkness; and the darkness comprehended it not. (John 1:1–5 KJV)

If space goes on and on forever, with no end, then why cannot *Life*? Or for that matter, even death? If God created the heavens and the earth and you, then you have to realize that you are nothing compared to a being that can do that. Maybe it is true that your pride and even your being is as filthy rags. Maybe in God's sight you have sinned, and your wages for that sin is eternal or forever lasting death—The Second Death[9].

Maybe you have been a fool for believing there is no God, believing the world is flat!

I have come to the conclusion that I do not have to rule out everything that science says, I just have to compare it with God's word. Science says it started with a big bang. In our conception of things, when God created the heavens and the earth, it could appear to us as a big bang. Science says it took billions of years for this or that to have happened. Peter, one of Jesus' disciples, told us not to be ignorant of one thing, that one day is with the Lord as a thousand years, and a thousand years as one day. I believe this is figurative and not literal. Just as Jesus used parables—examples of earthly things—to give us insight to spiritual things, I believe Peter could have used a day is as a million years and a million years as a day to God instead of using a thousand. Again I believe the Spirit was guiding Peter to let us not be ignorant by putting limits on God's time or his Power. If you take 1 year times 365 days times a thousand years you get 365,000 years. The same by a million and you get 365,000,000 years. The same by a billion and it is 365,000,000,000 years. You get the picture—where man and science says "X", in God's sight and time it could have been one day.

Not everything that science says and believes is totally false. After all they did finally come to the conclusion that the earth rotated around the sun and not the other way around. I have made my point; now let us go on to *Believing*.

Earlier in the chapter, I quoted man's definition of believing from the dictionary; now if the Bible is God's Holy inspired word, and in the beginning was the Word and the Word was with God, then you have to explore his word to find out what it says about *Believing.*

Thou believest that there is one God; thou doest well: the devils also believe, and tremble. (James 2:19 KJV)

Almost everyone has seen, heard or read John 3:16 before, but not necessarily the previous two verses or the next two verses.

And as Moses lifted up the serpent in the wilderness, even so must the Son of man be lifted up: That whosoever believeth in him should not perish, but have eternal life.

For God so loved the world, that he gave his only begotten Son, that whosoever believeth in him should not perish, but have everlasting life. For God sent not his Son into the world to condemn the world; but that the world through him might be saved.

He that believeth on him is not condemned: but he that believeth not is condemned already, because he hath not believed in the name of the only begotten Son of God. (John 3:14–18 KJV)

After Jesus had risen from the dead, Apostle Thomas said he would not believe without seeing; Jesus told him the following,

Then saith he to Thomas, **Reach hither thy finger, and behold my hands; and reach hither thy hand, and thrust *it* into my side: and be not faithless, but believing.** And Thomas answered and said unto him, My Lord and my God. Jesus saith unto him, **Thomas, because thou hast seen me, thou hast believed: blessed *are* they that have not seen, and *yet* have believed.** (John 20:27–29 KJV)

The Father loveth the Son, and hath given all things into his hand. He that believeth on the Son hath everlasting life: and he that believeth not the Son shall not see life; but the wrath of God abideth on him. (John 3:35–36 KJV)

For the Father judgeth no man, but hath committed all judgment unto the Son: That all *men* should honour the Son, even as they honour the Father. He that honoureth not the Son honoureth not the Father which hath sent him. Verily, verily, I say unto you, He that heareth my word, and believeth on him that sent me, hath everlasting life, and shall not come into condemnation; but is passed from death unto life. (John 5:22–24 KJV)

And this is the will of him that sent me, that every one which seeth the Son, and believeth on him, may have everlasting life: and I will raise him up at the last day. (John 6:40 KJV)

Verily, verily, I say unto you, He that believeth on me hath everlasting life. (John 6:47 KJV)

For I am not ashamed of the gospel of Christ: for it is the power of God unto salvation to every one that believeth; to the Jew first, and also to the Greek. For therein is the righteousness of God revealed from faith to faith: as it is written, The just shall live by faith. (Rom. 1:16–17 KJV)

WHAT IS FAITH?

Now faith is the substance of things hoped for, the evidence of things not seen. (Heb. 11:1 KJV)

Again, I could go on and on but it is my *prayer* that by now you have got the point that I am trying so desperately to make. The first step to any understanding of God's Word, and to an Everlasting Life with the Father, God, is *believing* in Jesus Christ as Lord and Savior of the world; only then can you have that same salvation.

No one can be saved until they *believe* in Jesus Christ and the Father that sent him. Believing in them makes you realize you are lost, and once you realize that, *you can be saved.*

Jesus himself said to John;

Behold, I stand at the door, and knock: if any man hear my voice, and open the door, I will come in to him, and will sup with him, and he with me. To him that overcometh will I grant to sit with me in my throne, even as I also overcame, and am set down with my Father in his throne. (Rev. 3:20–21 KJV)

Herein lies the end of chapter one and the beginning of chapter two. As I stated earlier in the book, Believing was the most difficult thing I had ever done in my life.

Salvation was the easiest thing I have ever received in my life!

Once I believed in my heart that Jesus Christ was the only begotten Son of God and that God had created the heavens and the earth and that I was therefore not the all knowing, all special person that I thought I was, then I knew that I must—according to his word—be lost and could therefore somehow be saved!

Salvation
Chapter 2

I am going to start this chapter by asking you to use your imagination again. This is a fairly easy picture to bring up in your mind. You have either seen it in person or pictures of it in one form of media or another.

There is a clear bright running river going over a dam, and at the dam are a power plant or generator and power lines running from the plant off into the distance. We know that at some point those power lines come into our homes and are controlled by a switch on the wall that turns on or off the light.

Now I am going to attempt to give you a parable, an earthly example which has a spiritual connotation.

Picture the running water as God, Jesus Christ, or the Word. Water is our life source. It is in this analogy the source of the power.[10]

The power plant and power lines are the Holy Spirit.[11]

The light switch on the wall is our brains or mind and the light is our hearts.[12]

Salvation is the second step in the circle which has its beginning in Christ and its ending in his Second Coming. As I quoted earlier in Chapter one and will only paraphrase here, Christ is the Word and was in the beginning with God. The Holy Spirit is the source of power he promised us and is his way of living in us and communicating with us.[11] Our minds or brains is the switch which controls whether we *Believe* and allows the Holy Spirit access to our hearts. And once we have accepted God's free gift,[13] our light will so shine that others can see Christ in us.[12]

I am going to repeat three things here that I said from chapter one to refresh your memory.

1. At one point in my life when I was seventeen I had tried accepting God and found out within a couple of weeks that was not real.

2. I now know, (not only believe), what is real.

3. I said I thought that if I could understand the Bible then maybe I could believe it. Once I Believed and got Saved, the Spirit started showing and explaining the scriptures to me in a way that made sense and I could understand.

Now for the explanation of these 3 items.

1. When I was seventeen I was living at home and working at a plant where both my Father and Mother worked. Just shortly before this I had been skipping school on a regular basis and thrown out of school over a foolish prank that got blown way out of proportion and got me arrested. I sat in jail and would not give them my name—remember at that time I thought I could handle anything.

   My girlfriend at the time told her parents, and they in turn called my parents, who came and got me out of jail around ten that night. I was glad to see them but I played it cool as though I didn't understand what the big deal was. I think my Dad's boss paid for my Dad to get an attorney, but before anything could be done, I up and ran away from home with two pennies in my pocket.

When I got to the shopping center by my house, I took the two pennies and bought four pieces of chewing gum, after all what good was only two cents going to do me. I hitch hiked and left New Orleans, headed for California, where I had a friend whose family had moved out there. I had called, and he said come on. Along the way, I would work odd jobs and once accepted help from a Salvation Army Representative in order to get a meal.

I made it to Albuquerque, NM before I got locked up again, this time for vagrancy. They placed me in a detention center for juveniles, and again I would not give them my name or any information and purposely did not have any ID. After about a week in the detention center, I got in a fight, and I finally had them call my parents. I found out that my friend's parents had called mine to let them know that I was headed to California. To shorten this story, Mom and Dad got me home and out of trouble and got me a job with them. I was making good money for the time and had decided that I was going to buy a brand new 1965 Marina Blue Corvette Stingray with solid white interior. My Dad was going to co-sign the papers, and we were at the dealership making the final arrangements when I told him to wait.

(Be, patient, there *is* a reason for this story!)

He did not understand, but I think he was relieved until the next Saturday. I told him I would talk to him about it later. The next Saturday morning I had worked out all the details and, while riding to work with him, laid the following on him.

If I could afford the payments on that Vette, my girl-friend and I could afford to get married, if he and Mom would let us live in my bedroom until we could save enough money to buy furniture and find an apartment. They discussed it, agreed to allow us to get married, and two Saturdays later we got married in a small church two blocks from the house. Everyone thought my girlfriend was pregnant because of us getting married that quickly, but my son was not born until eighteen months later. We had a daughter twenty-two months after that.

The earliest memory I have of my Dad was that every night, without exception, he would take his bath, lay down on the bed in his boxer shorts and A-Shirt, take his Bible off the night stand next to the bed, and start reading.

After my wife and I got married he told us, if we could go to church and get married, we were all going to start getting up and going to church every Sunday morning. It was there that I became concerned that I was going to hell because I was not saved.

One Sunday morning my wife and I went down the aisle during an alter call at the end of a service. The pastor prayed a prayer, and I got up feeling better and went on with my life for a couple of weeks. The pastor then preached a message on Abraham and Isaac, and I realized that I had not been saved, and instead of talking with the pastor, I just turned my mind off—shut the switch off—and would not consider anything else pertaining to God.

I didn't realize, until I was twenty-nine years old, that I did not go down the church aisle when I was seventeen to be saved; I went down looking to receive an insurance policy against going to hell.

2. I now know, (not only believe), what is real. When I got saved, God took away my heart of stone and replaced it. He made all things new, forgave me, and did away with the old.[14] My heart was transformed, and I became a new and different individual. I now not only *Believe* in God, I know he is real because he lives within my heart.

3. I thought that if I could understand the Bible then maybe I could believe it. Once I Believed and got Saved, the

Spirit started showing and explaining the scriptures to me in a way that made sense and I could understand.[15]

Salvation only requires three things, *Believing, Repentance, and Confession.*

Let me repeat that, being saved only requires three things of you, *Believing, Repentance, and Confession.* I will explain and go into detail shortly, but you cannot give anything up to be saved, you cannot do anything or any work to be saved, you cannot buy it, etc.

At seventeen I tried accepting God, but it was not until the age of twenty-nine that I started to truly question what I believed and had faith in.

What happened during those twelve years to completely turn me around? I will try to make it brief because how it happened is not the important thing, that it *did* is what counts. What road I took to town—or Jesus—does not matter, only that I realized that Jesus was the only way.

Jesus saith unto him, **I am the way, the truth, and the life: no man cometh unto the Father, but by me.** (John 14:6 KJV)

Within a year of getting married I was slated to be drafted during the Vietnam War, and so joined the Air Force instead. Later I was shipped to Alaska, went through a separation with my first wife, and eventually gave up a really good job making really good money at the time for a reconciliation with her—my choice. I moved back to what we called at the time the lower 48 states, went through bankruptcy and another separation. Going through a divorce, I started drinking heavier and using pot more than I ever had when off work. I was paying child support when I could barely make ends meet—of course, the drinking and the pot did not help to make ends meet and did not help me be a good Father either. In short, the total sum of my experiences started me to thinking that I was not really in control of anything in my life.

At the job I then had, there were a couple of Christian women; that invited me to visit their Church. One was married, and one was going through a divorce. I was interested in dating the one going through the divorce, but I didn't want to be too obvious and so I planned to go to the other lady's Church first, just for a couple of times. Once I started going to the other church, something very tragic happened to the woman I was interested in; she had a niece, her nephew's wife, and one of their twin sons killed in a car accident on the twins' birthday, which also happened to be my birthday.

A drunk driver ran a red light killing all three. One twin and a friend survived the crash. I was mad as anything or anyone—I had a real bad temper—but started noticing that all the family and the people at her Church were reacting differently than I was. I began to question my reaction versus theirs. How could they be so hurt and yet reacting with compassion and understanding beyond anything I had ever experienced? During the next month or so, I would go to Sunday School, morning and evening Worship Services on Sunday, Wednesday night Services, and to Brotherhood Meetings. All of this was just to impress—and date— this lady.

But I started noticing more and more that these people were different than anybody I had met and hung around with in the past. I started listening and observing and came to the conclusion that if there was a God that they all believed in, I had a bunch of questions that would have to be answered. I started thinking that, before I would go any further, I would have to understand the entire Bible and be sure that I could live the life that I was supposed to. If I understood the Bible then *maybe* I could *believe* it.

By now I had started dating this lady, and we would go places after the services on Sunday and various nights during the week. Then *this* happened; I jumped into my car one day, headed to Sunday School, and the radio was on, tuned—as usual—to a Rock-n-Roll Station. This station, on Sunday mornings, had a preaching service, and I would always change the station to my second favorite Rock-n-Roll Station. I was lighting a cigarette and could not push the button as soon as it came on, and at that moment the preacher made the following statement: *"Do not try and Believe the Bible by understanding it, but understand the Bible by Believing it."*

I pushed the radio button; my second favorite Rock-n-Roll Station came on, and I was off to see my lady friend, who I was starting to feel was my girlfriend.

Looking back on it now, it is funny! The first date I asked her out on, I told her to pick out anywhere she wanted to go, not to worry about the cost, and just tell me how to dress. She told me to dress just casual. I picked her up, and she took me to a Gospel Singing; I thought I was surrounded by a bunch of lunatics. The second date I told her was my choice, and I took her out to a nightclub to go dancing. We got a seat. I ordered a beer, and she told me to take her home or that she'd catch a cab. I never even got to taste my beer.

Little by little as time went by she would witness to me and tell me I just did not understand, and I would think to myself, *I understand perfectly, you're the one who doesn't understand.* But that Radio Preacher's words kept coming back to me, over and over. I was trying to *Believe* the Bible by understanding it—without the teaching of the Holy Spirit, I was not ever going to understand it.[15]

HOW THEN DID THIS CHANGE TAKE PLACE?

STEP ONE—BELIEVING

A jailer asked Paul and Silas, "…and said, Sirs, what must I do to be saved?" And they said, "Believe on the Lord Jesus Christ, and thou shalt be saved, and thy house." (Acts 16:30–31 KJV)

Note that there were no caveats or provisos in their answer. Not *maybe*, not *if you were predestined*, not *if you do some work.* Simply believe and thou shalt be saved.

And as Moses lifted up the serpent in the wilderness, even so must the Son of man be lifted up: That whosoever believeth in him should not perish, but have eternal life.

For God so loved the world, that he gave his only begotten Son, that whosoever believeth in him should not perish, but have everlasting life. For God sent not his Son into the world to condemn the world; but that the world through him might be saved.

He that believeth on him is not condemned: but he that believeth not is condemned already, because he hath not believed in the name of the only begotten Son of God. (John 3:14–18 KJV)

Jesus saith unto him, **I am the way, the truth, and the life, no man cometh unto the Father, but by me.** (John 14:6 KJV)

There is a way which seemeth right unto a man, but the end thereof *are* the ways of death. (Prov. 14:12 KJV)

But we are all as an unclean *thing*, and all our righteousnesses *are* as filthy rags; and we all do fade as a leaf; and our iniquities, like the wind, have taken us away. (Isa. 64:6 KJV)

For by grace are ye saved through faith; and that not of yourselves: *it is* the gift of God: Not of works, lest any man should boast. (Eph. 2:8–9 KJV)

For all have sinned, and come short of the glory of God (Rom. 3:23 KJV)

For the wages of sin *is* death; but the gift of God *is* eternal life through Jesus Christ our Lord. (Rom. 6:23 KJV)

When you accept that the intelligent designer, GOD, created the heavens and the earth and created you, then you must realize that you are nothing compared to him. He created you to fellowship with him, and he walked in the Garden of Eden with man, until man disobeyed him through sin. Man gained the knowledge of Good and Evil, and realized he was naked. The Lord God then made coats of skins to clothe them, and every man and woman since Adam and Eve have been conceived in the lust of the flesh, except the only begotten Son of God. *See Genesis 1–3* [16]

Once you *Believe*, that is the first step. Remember, even the devils believe.

Thou believest that there is one God; thou doest well: the devils also believe, and tremble. (James 2:19 KJV)

Once you allow the switch— in your mind—to be flipped to the on position and allow your heart to Believe; once you *BELIEVE* in Christ as the only begotten Son of God, you are then ready to accept God's word that you are lost and have been separated from his fellowship by sin and that *HIS* plan of Salvation was to have his only Son to die and be sacrificed for your sins[17] and raised from the dead the third day that you might have a way to regain that fellowship and the forgiveness of those sins which you have committed.

I mentioned what a difference the impression of several Christian people made on my life and thought process. Unfortunately you cannot look at the life of everyone who calls themselves a Christian as an example. I will cover that in detail in Chapter three. Too many people do the same thing that I did when I was seventeen and are looking for a Savior but leave out steps two and three of God's plan of Salvation.

STEP TWO—REPENTANCE

Again from my copy of the Webster Dictionary,

Repent *v.i.* to desire to change one's life as a result of sorrow for one's sins.

At this point I am assuming that you have decided to Believe in Jesus and are ready to repent. First let me say that some people tend or try to make a work out of repentance. Remember from previously mentioned scriptures that Salvation cannot come from any work or man would boast about it and it would be their doing instead of a gift of God by his Grace.

Jesus himself said, **"I came not to call the righteous, but sinners to repentance."** [18] And also; **"joy shall be in heaven over one sinner that repenteth, more than over ninety and nine just persons, which need no repentance."** [19]

Repentance is, in simple terms, changing your mind—turning that switch on again—and realizing that you are sorry for the way you have lived and that you want to change. You want to turn away from the things of this world and turn towards God and look to him to be not only your Savior but also Lord of your life. The problem with too many people is that they never reach the point of being sorry for the way they have treated God. They feel they are good people. I have heard, way too often, *I am just as good as so and so*, or *if they are a Christian I have nothing to worry about*, etc. Remember, according to his word, we have *all* sinned and *all* come short of his glory. And the wages or result of that sin is the second death or condemnation already for not believing in God's Son. I am no better than any other person on this earth. The only difference is that I was a sinner that has been forgiven by God's grace and I still commit sins of commission and omission and have to ask God's forgiveness.

In Chapter 1, I said being saved is simple and easy. Being saved is the easiest thing I have ever done in my life. Getting to the point where I could be saved is the most difficult thing I have ever done in my life. Salvation, to me, was free; it was a gift from God by his grace.[(13)] My Salvation was not free to God. It cost him his only Begotten Son. I did not have to pay anything for it, but Jesus paid it all; through his stripes, I was healed.[20] There were no works that I had to do, or could have done.[(13)] Jesus did all the work through his freely giving his life.[21]

In my mind, I allowed myself to *Believe* in Jesus as the only begotten Son of God and accepted that his word must be true and made more sense than evolution. In my mind, I accepted that his word must be the truth.[22] I believed in the Bible and trusted that God would help me to understand it if I would give him the chance. I finally had Faith, My first reference in the book.

Now faith is the substance of things hoped for, the evidence of things not seen. (Heb. 11:1 KJV)

I let the switch in my mind flip to the on position and allowed the Holy Spirit to let me know that Christ was at the door knocking.

Behold, I stand at the door, and knock: if any man hear my voice, and open the door, I will come in to him, and will sup with him, and he with me. To him that overcometh will I grant to sit with me in my throne, even as I also overcame, and am set down with my Father in his throne. (Rev. 3:20–21 KJV)

I realized according to his word—that I was now going to accept and believe—I was a sinner and needed to repent. I flipped the switch to on again and said in my mind, *Jesus I want you to not only be a Savior to me, I want you to be Lord of my Life and direct me in all things. I want the Salvation that your word promises me and I am willing to let your Spirit guide and direct my every path.* I had just *BELIEVED* and had just *REPENTED*. I had turned from the things or pleasures of this world and to God.[23] Now the only thing left was confession.

STEP THREE—CONFESSION

That if thou shalt confess with thy mouth the Lord Jesus, and shalt believe in thine heart that God hath raised him from the dead, thou shalt be saved. For with the heart man believeth unto righteousness; and with the mouth confession is made unto salvation. For the scripture saith, Whosoever believeth on him shall not be ashamed. (Rom. 10:9–11 KJV)

I cannot speak for anyone else and can only describe my own personal experience. It was Sunday morning at the end of worship on October 17, 1976. I was standing next to my Lady Friend about the third row from the back on the left hand side of the Church. Music was playing, and people were singing. I was contemplating letting go of the pew in front of me that I was holding on to and trusting in God. It felt as if the soles of my shoes were glued to the floor. I could not move! I then realized that something was holding me back, I did not know what it was. I then said in my mind, *Lord Jesus, Please forgive me and please save me, and I somehow found the strength to lift my right foot and step out into the aisle to go down and receive Christ.* In my mind, I had just confessed him as my personal Lord and Savior and agreed to repent and turn from the things of the world and turn my life over to him.

I have always felt there was a Gospel Song to be written about; The day I was saved there were two steps made. I made the first step away from my pride, and Jesus made the second step away from Heaven and to my side.

Again I cannot speak for anyone else, but his word tells us he will return for us in the twinkling of an eye.[24] In that same twinkling of an eye, my heart was changed. I went on down the aisle and met the preacher at the front. I remember seeing tears running down the face of the choir director, who had also been my Sunday School Teacher. I do not remember anything the preacher said other than when we stood up from praying he asked me if I had anything I wanted to say. I could not wait to tell everyone that Christ had saved me. I did not jump up and down or shout or anything similar to that. I just knew the difference from when I was seventeen and this time. We are all the total sum of our past experiences and react to the same Salvation from God in different manners. I just know that, whoever you are and whatever your makeup from your experiences, once God saves you,

you will not be ashamed. You are ready to confess him with your mouth to whoever will listen.

I always tell people, "Once you have been *saved*, you can do four things."

1. You can tell anyone where it happened. You may not know the exact street address. The church may get torn down and a mall built in its place. But you remember exactly where it happened. It may be that you knelt down next to a rock in a field, it may be that you were in your home next to a recliner, or in your bed, or in a car driving down the road. Wherever, you will always be able to tell where it happened.

2. You will always be able to tell when it happened. Between 12 and 12:30 on Sunday morning October 17, 1976. The only reason I can give you the *exact* date is because my lady friend gave me a Bible with it written in the front of it. If she had not done that, I would only be able to tell you that it happened one Sunday morning after Church Services. Again you will remember when it happened. Maybe not to the minute, or day, but you will always remember when it happened because you will have been changed and will have become a new person in Christ.

3. You will always be able to tell people what you did. You *BELIEVED* with your heart unto righteousness in Jesus and his Father that sent him, and that God has raised him from the dead and that he now lives. You *REPENTED* or turned from the World to Him, and you *CONFESSED* with your mouth unto Salvation that Jesus was now, not only your Savior, but Lord of your Life.

4. You will always be able to tell what God did. He was true to his word and not only *SAVED* you, but forgave all your sins, no matter what they may have been, and gave you a new heart and made all things new. That is right, no matter how large or how small your sins

may have been, no matter what they were, God forgave them and made all things new. He gave you a complete fresh start with everlasting life.

You can right now, wherever you are and whatever time it is—do the same thing and receive Salvation right this minute. His word tells us now is the time and now is the day of salvation.[25]

DO NOT WAIT! Do not finish reading the book; there will be time for that later, and it will mean more. Allow the switch in your mind to be turned on and *BELIEVE;* allow it to be turned on and *REPENT.* You may be a good person and have tried to live a good life, but none of our good deeds is enough, it took Christ's Sacrifice on the cross and his Resurrection from the grave. Right now in your own words, *pray out loud—CONFESS* with your mouth—just as you were talking to a friend, and say something similar but from your own heart as the following,

Father, in the name of Jesus Christ, I believe in you with all my heart. I believe Jesus is your only Begotten Son and that you raised him from the dead so that I might receive Salvation and be reunited with you. I repent of my sins, (whatever they might be), and I accept you as LORD and SAVIOR of my life.

That is it! You have been *SAVED.*

Now start going to a bible-believing, bible-preaching Church, and forsake not the assembling together of yourself with other fellow Christians.[26] I go to a Baptist Church because I believe it is the denomination that most closely follows the Bible. *ALSO ATTEND EVERY SERVICE AND ACTIVITY THAT YOU CAN.* It will help in your growth as a Christian and helps to fulfill the following two scriptures:

Study to shew thyself approved unto God, a workman that needeth not to be ashamed, rightly dividing the word of truth. But shun profane *and* vain babblings: for they will increase unto more ungodliness. (2 Tim. 2:15–16 KJV)

But sanctify the Lord God in your hearts: and *be* ready always to *give* an answer to every man that asketh you a reason of the hope that is in you with meekness and fear: (1 Peter 3:15 KJV)

I then understood what it was that my girlfriend was trying to tell me; she was right I truly hadn't understood before. After the gift of Salvation, God started working immediately in my life, thus all the praise that I give him. Several other things happened first. My then girlfriend and others could see the change in my life. Her name is Linda, and she and I were married on July 3, the following year. She has said that she would never have married me if I had not got Saved and changed the way I did. After thanks for Christ and my Salvation, second comes my thanks for his having brought her into my life and for the many wonderful years of marriage we have had since.

I still had many questions and was very unsure of myself. I did not want to do something that I should not or not to do something that I should. I said earlier that I am no better than any other person on this earth. The only difference is that I was a sinner that has been forgiven by God's grace, and I still commit sins of commission and omission and have to ask God's forgiveness.[27]

As your growth develops—*As a new Christian*—Keep in mind the following two scriptures.

Draw nigh to God, and he will draw nigh to you… (James 4:8 KJV)

Rejoice evermore. Pray without ceasing. In every thing give thanks: for this is the will of God in Christ Jesus concerning you. Quench not the Spirit. Despise not prophesyings. Prove all things; hold fast that which is good. Abstain from all appearance of evil. (1 Thess. 5:16–22 KJV)

Sometimes it is hard to understand God's will for our life, and having patience to wait on him to answer a prayer is one of my weaknesses.

I am going to end this chapter with another joke that I have heard. It reminds us that we have to be careful to listen to that still small voice.²⁸

Once there was a violent hurricane coming and the authorities were going around warning everyone to evacuate their homes. The sheriff came to this one house, and there was an elderly man sitting in his rocker on the front porch. The sheriff got out and told him he needed to evacuate and go to the shelter they had prepared for everyone. The elderly man proceeded to explain to the sheriff that he trusted in the Lord with all his faith and was going to stay in his home; The Lord would take care of him. The sheriff tried his best to talk the man out of staying, but to no avail, and went on to warn others. Later, sure enough, all the streets were flooded, and the rescue squad came along in their boat going up and down streets to rescue people and bring them to the shelter which was safe and on high ground. They came to the man's house that the sheriff had told them about. He thanked them for their concern but assured them that his Lord was going to take care of him. Later the water had rose very high and the man had cut a hole through his roof from the inside and was sitting on the very top of his house. The coast guard was flying missions looking for anyone that might still be alive. They came upon the man and lowered a basket to lift the man to safety. He shouted up to them to go on and rescue someone that needed it, his Lord was going to take care of him. Reluctantly they flew on. After the man perished and was standing before the Lord he said, "I do not understand. You promised to never leave or forsake me." The Lord looked at him and said. "My Son, what more did you want? I sent the sheriff, the rescue squad and the coast guard, and you ignored them all."

The Lord does promise to never leave or forsake us,²⁹ and at times it is difficult to understand his good and acceptable and perfect will in our lives,³⁰ after all, good things happen to bad people, and bad things happen to good people. But we should follow the advice Paul gave to the young Ephesian Christians:

Speaking to yourselves in psalms and hymns and spiritual songs, singing and making melody in your heart to the Lord; Giving thanks always for all things unto God and the Father in the name of our Lord Jesus Christ. (Eph. 5:19–20 KJV)

Thus the continuation of Chapter 3, Praise.

Praise
Chapter 3(b)

When first Saved, I needed God's help in resolving several issues. The first bunch of issues I am going to group all together, the same worries or concerns that almost everyone has, and that is making a living, food, shelter, clothing, etc. The second was tithing, the third was drinking and drugs and a fourth that I did not understand at the time and that I needed God's help with.

The first Sunday after I was saved, my future sister-in-law sang a song titled *Thank you Lord for your Blessings on me* by James, Russell and Ed Easter—The Easter Brothers. The lyrics brought several scriptures to mind; over the years the Holy Spirit has shown me others along the same lines. In a nutshell these lyrics and scriptures assured me that I did not have to worry about Food, Clothing or Shelter, for God was going to take care of me. I just needed to be thankful and give him the praise. I still needed to work, for even the ants have to work, but I was not ever going to have to beg for bread. [31]

The second concern I had was tithing. My job at that time was manager over a small manufacturing plant of about sixty employees. I mentioned earlier that I was just barely making ends meet. I had heard during some of my attendance to Sunday School, Preaching and Brotherhood meetings that I should tithe, which is to say give ten percent to God's storehouse.[32] Even without the drinking and pot, there was no way I could give ten percent of what I made to the

Church, or so I thought. I now realize that you can never out give God. I started praying about it. Remember I got Saved on October 17th. Around the first week or two in November, my boss came to me and was discussing all the aspects of the upcoming budget for the new year. He told me the following, "We are well pleased with the job you have been doing for us, and go-ahead and put into the budget a ten percent increase for yourself."

I almost fell out of my chair. Not the six or seven percent they were giving the employees, not twelve or fifteen percent—but a ten percent increase. I said, "Thank You," (and in my mind, *Praise the Lord*), and started tithing my salary increase with the very first check. The Lord kept blessing me through the years, and at some point I realized he meant for me to give of the first fruits of my labor—not from my net but gross salary.[33] Even later I came to realize that I was not making an offering to the Lord until it was over and above the tithe or ten percent that I was *suppose* to give.

But this *I say*, He which soweth sparingly shall reap also sparingly; and he which soweth bountifully shall reap also bountifully. Every man according as he purposeth in his heart, *so let him give*; not grudgingly, or of necessity: for God loveth a cheerful giver. And God *is* able to make all grace abound toward you; that ye, always having all sufficiency in all *things*, may abound to every good work (2 Cor. 9:6–8 KJV)

In other words, I have never giving anything to the Lord or given it in his name that he has not more than repaid in his gracious blessings. He has made my cup run over.[34]

The third big concern I had was that I wanted to get ahead in business, getting promotions, etc. I knew that the company would hold business meetings at hotels a lot of the times or have business dinners, and there was always drinking. I did not see anything wrong with it as a new young Christian. I knew there were scriptures warning against strong drink and wine and its ability to deceive, but I would only be socially drinking with the bosses and not getting drunk, and I did not see the harm.[35] I thought I could handle it and that by having a drink with them it would not make me an outcast, always having to explain myself. But I also knew the scripture to abstain from all appearance of evil, so I decided to pray about it and let God give me the answer. Until he answered, I would not drink and had quit the pot. November went by, and in December the company had a Christmas party for its management—a real nice dinner with all the drinks anyone wanted. I did not drink and explained to a couple of people who had known me for some time that I had been saved and was not drinking. They politely changed the subject and went on being themselves. I felt uncomfortable and out of place. New Year's Eve came along and another party. I really felt out of place and blamed it on the not drinking. From the age of fourteen, I had drunk, especially on the weekends, and I knew I could handle it and you could have a better time when you were drinking—*or so I thought*.

Still I decided that I was not going to, until God gave me an answer to my prayer.

In February the company got bought out by a larger company, and they were having their annual meeting for all the plant managers and human resource managers in either late February or early March. There would be a couple hundred people at this meeting, and I was going to get to meet all the higher-ups. The night before the meeting, there was to be a social hour with hors d'oeuvres and a free bar. I thought, *Oh great, just what I need, my big chance to meet all the big wigs and I have got to explain why I am the only one in the place not drinking.* Something told me inside, *you remember the little lapel pin that your Sunday School Teacher gave you for Christmas. It is a cross! If you wear that, surely no one will try and push drinks off on you, and you will not have to explain a thing.* I drove to the city where the meeting was to be held, and my immediate boss, the Vice President of our division happened to be driving up at the same time. We met and he started out by saying, "I heard you just recently got Saved."

"Yes sir," I said.

He then replied, "Good, God will never let you down."

I felt a little better about the whole thing now. We went ahead and checked in, and later I got dressed to go down to the room where the social hour was being held. Upon walking in, I got a coke and started talking with some of the managers I knew from our old company. A little later this man came up, introduced himself by name only, and started the conversation off with my cross lapel pin. I explained to him that I had just recently been Saved. It was my first meeting with the new company, and I did not know a lot of the people there and would have felt uncomfortable with people shoving drinks at me all night. So I decided to wear it. We talked for a good long while and then parted ways. Not long after, the social hour was over, and they closed the free bar, and everyone dispersed. A lot of the people just moved on to the bar, but I went up to my room.

The next morning I went down to the meeting, found my place, had a seat, and waited to see what it was all about. There was a bunch of information on how the company had done the past year and welcoming the new company as part of the team, etc. There were several guest speakers, some funny, some not. We broke for lunch, and then the meeting started up again. The President of the company introduced the next guest speaker and out walked the man I had the long conversation with during the social hour. He was a big shot with a really large company. He started out by explaining that when he is invited to be a guest speaker with a company the first thing he does is look up the financial information about the company and any other information he can gather. He then went on to say that last night he met one of the young new managers with the company—a young man named Bill Savage—who had just recently accepted Christ as his personal Lord and Savior and who spoke highly of his new company and everything they had done so far. He knew then that, with bright young mangers like that, the company would be alright. I do not remember much of what he said after that.

God had answered my prayer to my absolute astonishment, in a way that I just could not believe. By not drinking, standing up for Christ with a simple statement of a lapel pin, and discussing my Salvation with this complete stranger, I had just received more recognition than I would have ever gotten any other way. And just think of the recognition and honor that Christ received in this room full of unbelievers. All the higher-ups in the company had just heard my name associated with my Lord and Savior. I heard about it from different managers within the new company for months.

Here it was less than five months since I had been Saved, and I had received assurance that I no longer had to worry about my existence. I had received an answer to my prayer about tithing in the form of a raise enabling me to give my tithes, and God had answered my prayer about drinking in a fashion which gave me more recognition than I would have received any other way. You might not, but I sure give the Lord the Praise! There is a fourth thing that I needed help with from the Lord but did not understand it at the time; I am going to explain *that* a little later on.

Linda and I were engaged to be married on Sunday July 3, 1977. My boss came in one day and told me to come to the office. He had some good and some bad news. The bad news was that they were closing the small manufacturing portion of the plant that I was manager over. The good news was that until July he wanted me to go back and forth to a plant about forty miles away and help the manager there with a lot of new construction and remodeling they were doing. He also wanted me working with their Divisional Office Manager to develop a new inventory system that would fit both our companies needs and help draft the new companies policies and procedures. He wanted me to take complete charge of all the work being done, leaving the manager free to run the plant. He wanted it all wrapped up by July and an inventory taken and finished by Saturday July 2nd.

Then he offered myself and Linda new jobs, in positions being created as the Training Director and Training Supervisor for the entire division. It would mean salary increases for us both, but we would have to move from plant to plant to set up the programs, starting with the opening of a new plant in a nearby city. Linda and I would be starting out our married life with a few pots and pans, a few dishes, a bedroom set and an old hatchback Vega. We prayed for guidance in terms of the new jobs, especially since Linda had never been away from home except for a vacation, and we knew the Vega would not take that kind of traveling; in the end we accepted. We were given a company car in recognition of the traveling we'd be doing, and a consultant was hired to work with us and teach us the new program we would be using. Everything was set.

We would take the inventory, finish up Saturday evening, then Linda and I would be married on Sunday and would spend our honeymoon moving to the plant where we would start our training in Pennsylvania. We would spend one month there, and then move back to North Carolina and oversee the start-up hiring and begin the training of new operators and supervisors. Well the best laid plans—as the saying goes—soon went awry. Saturday afternoon rolled around and we were nowhere near finished the inventory. The outside auditors were delayed and could not make it to the plant until Sunday morning, and we were being married at 2:00 PM on Sunday. I *HAD* to be with the auditors, since I was instrumental in the development of the new inventory forms. Well, we worked late Saturday night, finished the inventory, and met the auditors on Sunday morning. Luckily we had done the inventory right and had double checked everything, for we only had until noon to clear the inventory before we had to leave for the wedding. We finished the audit, locked up at noon, loaded my parents and children in the car, drove to where we were married, drove to my sister-in-law's house for the reception, and were off on our honeymoon just as planned. We laughed about it for years within the company.

The plant in Pennsylvania was closed for the week of the fourth for vacation, so we had a week to get there. We took our time, went up the Blue Ridge Parkway and Skyline Drive, visited Washington DC, and made it in to our new home on Saturday just as planned. Not only that, the company paid our meals and lodging for three nights since we were moving on company business and also paid for the gas. When we arrived they had rented us half of a furnished trailer but that is a different story. The point of this story is that we went from having jobs we felt secure in to a complete unknown, and the Lord was in every detail and worked everything out. We found a small Baptist Church to attend for the month we were there, and one of the ladies at the plant had been a tour leader in the past, and her and her husband took my wife and I on a couple of tours through the Amish countryside, giving us details and taking us places we would never have seen otherwise. We also got to tour Philadelphia, seeing the Franklin Museum, Independence Hall, and the Liberty Bell, only to mention a few. After the month was up, as planned, we moved back to North Carolina.

We were only about an hour's drive away from my wife's home and my children, and they got to stay with us a lot. The Lord again led us to a small Bible Preaching Baptist Church, and we got to visit our home Church very often. We were doing okay, but with all the traveling back and forth—and my children with us often—it was very tight in the money department.

Before my wife and I started dating, she had bought some land from her parents and was making payments, which enabled them to retire and have sufficient income. After the Lord's tithes, my child support and that payment were going to be made before anything else.

One month it was especially tight, and we did not know what we were going to do. A man called and said he needed to meet with us pertaining to the land my wife owned and a right of way that cut through the property. We set up an appointment at our apartment the next night. My wife knew there was a pipeline running across the property but not much else. He arrived and started to explain that they were going to have to dig up the area beside the existing pipeline and lay another one. They did not need any additional right of way and they had the right to do this under the existing right of way terms, but since they were going to be digging it up they would level it back off, re-seed the area with grass, place straw over it and because they were doing this, they were going to give us two thousand dollars for any inconvenience it might cause. Now understand that we are talking about eleven acres of grown up, undeveloped property. I cannot begin to explain what those two thousand dollars meant to us and especially at that time. *Again Praise the Lord!*

It is along here that I realized what a truly wonderful wife the Lord had blessed me with. The morning of September 18th rolled around and I got up and gave my wife her Birthday Card and a small but inexpensive gift. She opened the gift; then the card, carefully reading every word. I spent a lot of time selecting the perfect card for I wanted it to be special for her first birthday with our being together. She thanked me, gave me a big hug and kiss. Then she says in a *real sweet voice*; there is only one thing. The 18th is your first wife's birthday; mine was on the eighth. I've never mixed them up again!

The plant was started very successfully, with our consultant's help. This was the man I spoke of in chapter one, the one who used the example of not going to the top of the mountain the first day when learning to ski. Our first anniversary we spent moving to our next assignment in Mississippi, just a few miles from my brother. Our second anniversary we spent moving to eastern North Carolina to yet another plant. By now, my son was living with us, and I was hoping my daughter would be soon as well. We were living in an apartment, and were now about a four and a half hour drive from home. I am not going to go on and on about my jobs, but I do want to explain and give the Lord the Praise where due. After several months of my wife and I setting up the training program and working with and training instructors and supervisors in the new method of training, the manager of the plant quit to go into business for himself. I was promoted to production manager of this large facility, and my wife was asked to start up and supervise a small manufacturing unit within the plant.

We were now settled and could join the church we had been attending and had a place we could count on being permanent, at least for awhile. We started looking to buy a house but realized rather quickly that without a down payment saved up it was not looking promising. The bank had one home that a man had let go back. His father had passed away, and he had moved into his father's house. It needed a lot of work, and we did not have the money to fix it up. Guess what? Another phone call; this time from my wife's family. A power company was coming through and buying up an additional right of way, and two of her sisters were going to lose their homes. My wife's family was always close, and six of the eight children had homes all around the old home place, which had been built by my wife's grandfather in 1907. We contacted the power company and offered to sell them the eleven acres my wife owned for them to move her sister's homes onto. Without going into all the details, it all worked out, and we received enough money to purchase the home we were looking at and do all the remolding that needed to be done, and her sister's homes were moved. They are happier where they are now located than they were before, and her parents were able to continue receiving their check for retirement.

In less than five years the Lord had answered several specific prayers and gave me a wife that I am still happily married to and that has been an excellent mother to my two children. He settled us in a wonderful small town and gave us a beautiful home. In addition to that he led us to a church where we felt at home and where he started using and training me through his Holy Spirit. First they ask me to be on the finance committee, then to be an assistant teacher to the adult class. Imagine me, at this early stage of my Christian life, being asked to teach adults who had known the Lord for many more years than I had. It really made me study and pray each week. The next year I was ask to teach a class from a home of mentally challenged individuals that our bus ministry picked up. They taught and gave me more love and understanding than I was ever able to return. Next I was asked to be the Sunday School Director.

It was here, in the early '80s, that God told me to write this book. When I say *told*, I do not mean that I heard a voice or anything like that; it is just that one day I knew he meant for me to do this. To me, at that time of my Christian growth, it was like an epiphany to me that God's plan for our lives was simply a complete circle. We Believed, we were Saved, and we were to give him the Praise and honor so that in turn other people would see Christ through us and Believe and so goes the circle. His plan for our lives was so simple, I felt like he wanted me to put it in writing so others could see. I convinced myself that there was no way. I understood what he was saying about our Praise through good works and teaching all things which he has commanded us[36] in order to inspire others to seek out his Son and receive Salvation through his grace in a recurring cycle until his second coming. But English was my worst subject in school, and I knew I was not qualified to write a book. This tug of war went on within for approximately thirty years.

During this approximate thirty year period, God continued to bless us through several more job promotions and eventually to owing our own successful business. He blessed us with several beautiful homes, cars and a boat etc. He blessed us during the many occasions we traveled and enjoyed this great country, which He created and blessed for all Americans.

Someone once told me that he simply could not understand how our forefathers, over two hundred years ago, could write such a far-reaching document as our constitution that is still relevant today and still guides the greatest nation on earth. My answer to him was simple. Our country was founded on the freedom of religion and being able to worship God, and God inspired man, through the Spirit, to write the Bible, so writing the constitution was, by comparison, a piece of cake. I said I was not going to make any more political comments, but I cannot resist just one more. I personally believe that America's problems today are as a result of our taking God out of everything and forgetting that our great nation was founded on the belief that "In God We Trust!"

The Bible explains that as new Christians we are as babes and must start out on the milk of the word.[37] Through study and practicing what the Bible teaches us, we gradually grow until we are ready for the meat of the word. I tease and kid with people a lot and have told them that I feel I have probably gone off milk and even the strained version of baby food, but at times feel like I am still on the baby food that has a few small chunks in it. I say this because I still feel inadequate in writing this. I do not have any problem telling and explaining to anyone what God has done for me and how he saved me. I do not have any problem sharing my testimony with anyone who will listen. What I have such a hard time with is that people tell me how much of a blessing I am to them when, in fact, it is they who are blessings to me.

I have used the example many times in teaching that, God gave us a book that has the instructions for how he wants us to live, but he gives us the free will to go about our daily lives choosing what we will do each day. Someone put together that the word BIBLE could be an acronym for Basic Instructions Before Leaving Earth. We have the free will to follow those instructions or not. But I have also said that if God is calling you to do something, you had better go ahead and do it. He will keep turning you in one direction or another until you obey and do it, and if you are not careful you might end up in the belly of a great fish; Jesus pointed out that Jonas (Jonah) was in the belly of a whale for three days and three nights.[38] Well I disobeyed God for almost thirty years. He kept turning me left and right and finally sent me a clear message that he meant for me to write this book giving him the Praise for all the things he had done for me in my life. Thus I will start with the Praise and testimony that most people are usually interested in hearing.

In the latter part of 1998, we were running the retail store God had blessed us with during the busy Christmas Season. I was not feeling well but did not pay it much attention as I had always been the picture of health and was very athletic. There were some problems going on within our family, but I was doing the best I could to handle all the pressure that was on me and to keep up my usual upbeat disposition and personality. One Saturday morning in mid January, I was feeling really bad but went ahead and got ready for work and drove the forty-five minutes to our store. My wife usually came in later and closed up if it was a slow day. When I arrived at the parking lot, I parked in our usual spot, got out, and started walking towards the building. About half way I had to sit down in the lot and catch my breath.

I got up, went back to the car, and called my wife and told her she would have to hurry and come down and open the store. I was headed back home and just could not make it that day. While driving home I realized that it was like I was in slow motion, cars would zoom around me blowing their horns and giving me funny looks and gestures. I then realized that I was only driving about 20 mph in a 45 mph zone. I kept feeling worse to the point I pulled over on the side of the road, put the car out of gear, and laid down in the front seat hoping someone would stop and call an ambulance for me. After laying there for some time with no one stopping, I pushed open the front door and just lay in the seat knowing someone would pass and see me in the seat and stop to help. No one did! After some time, I got up and started driving again trying very hard to keep a watch on myself and drive close to the speed limit. By God's grace, I made it home and called my wife and told her I was going to bed. At two the next morning, I woke my wife and told her to call an ambulance—something was drastically wrong.

What happened next was almost comical. First no emergency vehicle could find our house; not the ambulance, not the police, not the fire departments. I told my wife to call someone. She called her brother-in-law next door, and he went out to the road and flagged down the police. The fire department arrived shortly thereafter, inquiring what the problem was. I told them I did not know, I was hurting in my back and could not breathe. They checked my blood pressure and pulse and about that time the ambulance showed up with paramedics, more firemen and police. They ask me again what was wrong. Telling them the same thing, they hooked me up to an electrocardiogram, said my heart was okay, and asked if I wanted to be transported to the hospital or just wait and go see the doctor the next day. I told them they had to take me to the hospital; I was dying.

Getting the stretcher into our bedroom and out through the back porch was a job, but they finally did and loaded me in the ambulance. We sat there and sat there, and I ask them what they were waiting on. The attendee explained that with our long narrow drive all the police and fire trucks had them blocked in and they all had to back out of our drive before they could get out. When he reached the end of our drive he turned left instead of right—the road going directly to the hospital was a half block to the right. I explained this to him, and he informed me that they had to go the way they knew, which was about 10 miles out of the way.

During the ride, I asked if I was having a heart attack, and was told I wasn't according to the EKG. Upon arriving at the emergency room, I overheard the conversation between the paramedics and the hospital staff; they were buried with cases and the paramedic told the nurse that I was complaining of back pain and shortness of breath and probably had indigestion. They proceeded to take me off the stretcher and put me into a wheelchair and roll me to the triage nurse's station. She then asked me the same questions the paramedics had, did her job excellently, and rolled me out into the lobby to wait until they could see me. At 4:30 in the morning, I told my wife to go find a nurse and tell them I was dying in the lobby, sitting in one of their wheelchairs.

About fifteen to twenty minutes later a nurse came out to get me. She had my wife roll me back and they asked me to get up on a stretcher in the hall, for all their rooms were full. As I was trying to get up on the stretcher, she asked me what seems to be the problem. I had finally had enough.

"Nurse," I said politely as I could, "I have told the firemen, I have told the paramedics, I have told the triage nurse, and now I am telling you—soon I suppose I will tell a doctor—*I am dying*, and you have got to do something."

She instructed some man to get an EKG, and when it arrived, they hooked me up to it. It did not take long before the nurse took off at a run. She came flying back and they rolled the stretcher to an area that was not really a room and pulled a curtain around the area. In came a doctor and he said, "Mr. Savage I need you to remain calm. We are going to do everything we can for you, but you are in the middle of an AMI—acute myocardial infarction; you are having a heart attack."

They began sticking me with needles, having me chew aspirins, and hanging all kinds of bags with medicine in them on poles. The last thing I remember is looking over at my wife and saying a short prayer, *Lord, please take care of Linda.*

When I came to I was looking up at my feet and the light in the ceiling. The medicines they had given me had caused my blood pressure to drop, and I had blacked out. They had lifted the foot of the stretcher to make blood rush to my brain. I did not have an out-of-body experience or anything like that. It was just the most peaceful feeling I had ever had in my life, laying there, looking at my wife, and feeling the peace of God—knowing that, no matter what, we were both going to be okay!

Later that day, a doctor came into the intensive care unit and told my wife and I that I had suffered a massive heart attack but that the extent of the damage would not be known for another twenty-four hours. I had been given clot busters and other medications, but there would need to be a battery of tests run before their effectiveness could be determined.

The next day he returned to inform us that I had suffered only very minor damage to a small area of my heart. I had a 98% blockage in the artery they call the widow-maker—how's that for a nice nickname—and they had placed a stent in it; I would be fine.

End of story, right? Not quite so simple.

I was given diet instructions and told to join a rehab center for patients having suffered heart attacks. My insurance would not cover it, so I joined the local Y and started gradually lifting weights and swimming. Believe it or not, I went to Church services that first Wednesday night.

Six months later, I was in the Walmart attached to the mall our store was in, and they had a booth set up to check cholesterol. I was feeling great but thought I would have my cholesterol checked just to see how it was going. While they were filling out the paperwork, they asked me if I wanted a PSA test for prostate cancer. I said no, but then something told me, *you know your dad had it; you had better get checked.* I told the lady that I had changed my mind and to go ahead with the PSA test; I was not but fifty-two at the time, and dad had been in his seventies when he had prostate cancer, but it was not that expensive, so what the heck.

A week or two later I received a card in the mail with all the results and a comment to take the results to my doctor *immediately.* I knew the cholesterol results were good, way better than they had been, so I got on the internet to find out everything I could about the PSA results. It did not look good, so I called and made an appointment with my Veterans Administration Doctor.

The news was not good; it was prostate cancer! They were going to do a biopsy, and we would go from there. They did a complete bone scan, CAT scan, MRI, and I believe every test that was conceivable to man to ensure that the cancer had not metastasized to any other parts of my body.

All the test results looked good, even in the biopsy they did not find any cancer. So we would wait and see and keep doing PSA test every three months. Each test came back worse and worse. They keep doing biopsies and they keep coming back negative and my PSA keep getting worse. Needless to say my church was praying for me.

My doctor was getting concerned enough that he wanted to do a procedure in an attempt to find the cancer. It would require putting me in the hospital, hopefully for an outpatient surgery, but it was going to require me to have a catheter for a week or so. I was really, really dreading this procedure and did not know if I would be able to stand the catheter. Nonetheless he scheduled it for April 1, 2003.

I went in the hospital that morning. The doctor came and spoke with me for a bit, then they proceeded to put me to sleep and went ahead with the procedure. In the recovery room, I had been asleep longer than they wanted. I awoke to a nurse shaking me and calling my name, "Mr. Savage, Mr. Savage wake up..."

I became aware of where I was and what I had gone in for. Surprisingly, I did not feel the catheter and was relieved.

In my half-awake state I asked the nurse, "Why do have I a catheter?"

With a somewhat puzzled look she said, "Didn't the doctor explain the procedure to you, Mr Savage?

"Yes," I said, "but I came in for hemorrhoid surgery."

She turned pale as a ghost. "April Fools," I said.

She laughed halfheartedly and left the room. My niece, who is a registered nurse said, "Uncle Bill, you know that a nurse can kill you and not leave a trace, and if it had been me, I might have."

It is here that I need to interject a short testimony of my wife's.

On the Sunday morning of December 14, 2003 I came out of my Sunday School Class and the whole Church was a buzz. Linda had gotten Saved. I was shocked! I found her and ask what was going on. She proceeded to explain that when she was eleven she had gone down the church aisle; believing in God and Jesus but that the preacher had prayed and she just realized that she had never repented and ask God personally to forgive her. As a direct result of her courage in listening to the Holy Spirit and her testimony, two other men in our church who had led Christian lives accepted the Lord and were Saved. One has since been called to preach. All I could do was apologize to her for not asking about her Salvation, I just always assumed because of her lifestyle and her witnessing to me that she had been Saved. I tell this not to make anyone doubt their Salvation, but to give God the praise and reiterate that anyone that has been Saved can do the four things I mentioned in Chapter 2. I know the date because I returned the favor and wrote it in the front of her Bible.

Returning to the PSA tests and biopsies; they went on until May 2004. During that time I had a couple more heart attacks and stents numbers two and three put in. In May 2004, a biopsy came back positive for cancerous cells, meaning I needed surgery.

At this time I was treasurer of our Church and had keys to get in. I had been to the altar several times, praying to God about the whole thing. This time I went by myself and sat back in the third row from the back, where I had met the Lord and he had Saved me. I sat there begging God to heal me; he knew I would give him all the praise and that I did not want to go through the surgery. In addition to treasurer I was also an assistant teacher for the young people's class during Sunday School. The teacher gave me a book written by a lady who had survived cancer and battled with it for years. I do not like to read much, other than the Bible and thought, *great, how could this book possibly relate to what I am going through?* Of course, I did not tell him that, and out of respect for him as a dear friend and a fellow Christian, I thanked him and told myself I would have to read it.

It was difficult, and all through the book I was having problems understanding why I was reading it at all. Towards the end the writer wrote one sentence which made the entire book worth reading. She realized that if God did not heal her of her cancer here on this earth, he would heal her when she received her glorified body[39] but that he *would* heal her. That was what God meant for me to read.

That same month, my brother, who was six years younger than me, was told he had prostate cancer and that it had spread to his spine and leg and that he had less than six months to live. He finally succumb to the disease and went home to be with the Lord in August 2008, almost four and a half years later. Praise the Lord, for those extra years, for they gave me time to make several trips out to Utah to see him and discuss his Salvation with him.

Back to May 2004. The urologist who was going to do my surgery wanted to first remove several lymph nodes to ensure the cancer had not spread; that would mean more tests. He met with us one afternoon, scheduling us his last appointment so he could spend as much time with us as required and address any concerns we might have.

After an hour or so, he asked if we had any more questions. I told him that I saw his diploma from med-school hanging on the wall but that I thought it ought to be a law that physicians had to hang-up their report cards and grades as well. I did not want anyone cutting on me who had graduated medschool with a D minus. He burst out laughing, assured me he had finished in the top of his class, and offered any references I wanted. He then added that if you stop and think about it—which he never had—half of the doctors finished in the bottom half of their class.

After the surgery to remove the lymph nodes, everything went well, and they discharged me from the hospital the next day. Things went good for a day or two, but then on Monday I became very sick and had no idea what was wrong.

By now I had been going through tests and biopsies for five years. I was getting sicker and sicker and had Linda call an ambulance. This time they found our house with no problem; 911 had made us change our address after the incident in 1999. They took me to the hospital, admitted me, and proceeded to try and find out what was wrong with me. They did more test and more tests. They found out my gall bladder was full of gall stones, but that was not the problem and they did not know what was.

By this time I was having what my preacher calls a pity party. I was really sick and pitying myself and had no idea what was going on. Wednesday night it was decided that I needed a laxative. They gave me seven—yes seven—bottles of laxative during the night, one about every hour, and by the next morning I was so sick I knew I was going to die. I refused to take the morning medications they were trying to give me. I told them I had no idea what doctor was in charge or what the laxatives and medications were for and that I was not taking anything else until someone could tell me who was in charge and what they were trying to do. A little later a doctor came to see me and seemed very agitated that I dare question what they were doing. I explained everything including the laxatives I had been given despite the fact that I had barely eaten in a week. She was on duty for the doctor who had been treating me—that I had supposedly met—and assured me they would not do anything else without explaining it first.

Linda went home to take a bath and change her clothes around 10:30 Thursday morning. Shortly thereafter, a nurse walks in and says, real cheerfully, "Mr. Savage, how are you doing today?"

That did it, I burst out crying like a baby and told her they were letting me die in the hospital and nobody cared if I was getting any better or worse. She came over to me, took my hand and said, "Mr. Savage, do you mind if I pray with you?"

I thought to myself, *Lady, if you do not know Jesus Christ as your personal Savior, it is not going to do one bit of good for you to pray for me.* But something inside said, *Bill, shut your mouth and let her pray,* so I told her that would be fine.

She came around to the other side of the bed, pulled up a chair, let down the rail on the right side of the bed, and took my right hand in hers. "Father," she said (and I am getting teary-eyed just writing this), "I come to you in the name of Jesus Christ on behalf of Mr. Savage. He is having a really bad time and needs to feel your presence. I pray that within the hour you will let him know that you are with him, looking over him, and that he will be feeling better. Amen."

When she stood up, I purposely looked directly at her name tag; it read TINA, in all capital letters. I could not believe that a hospital would let a nurse pray that type of prayer, and I wanted to send her a card, thanking her and send one to her supervisor letting them know how sweet she was without telling them about her prayer, for I did not want to get her in any trouble.

At around 11:15 my pastor and his wife came to visit me. I was setting up on the side of the bed, laughing and joking with them and telling them about this nurse's prayer when the door cracked open, and Tina stuck her head in. She said she was leaving and just wanted to check in and make sure I was doing fine. I invited her in, introduced her to my pastor and his wife, and then she turned and left.

Almost immediately after Tina left, Linda opened the door and came in. She put down her purse and began to speak to our pastor and his wife. I asked her to go out to the nurses' station and get the last name of Tina, the nurse she passed on her way in. Linda said she did not pass a nurse on her way in. I told her to go out and get Tina's last name so I could send her a card. Linda went to the nurses' station and when she got there they informed her that they had no nurses named Tina, that there was no one on loan to that floor, and that they had no volunteers working at that time. They had no idea who this Tina was, but she was not from the hospital.

After returning with this information I described Tina to my wife and sent her back to the nurses' station to make sure, and she received the same response! There is not a doubt in my mind that the Lord sent an Angel[40] to remind me that he would never leave nor forsake me[(29)] and to pull me out of my pity party and to heal whatever was wrong with me. Friday morning my regular doctor came by to check on me, and I was up shaving, and he said, "You look better than on Monday when I saw you."

I informed him that I was fine, and I was getting ready to go home as soon as I could get ready, Praise the Lord! They never did find out what was wrong with me.

On August 13, 2004, I had the surgery, and in February my PSA starting going back up again. My urologist had told me, at the time of the surgery, that the cancer was not contained but that he hoped he had gotten it all. It was now apparent that he had not. He informed me that there was nothing they could do but give me hormone treatments in an effort to slow it down; radiation would not help.

Keep in mind that my brother and I were now talking on the phone every week, and I knew the pain and problems he was going through. I had a regular doctor's visit coming up with my VA primary care doctor, and after discussing it with him, he made an appointment for me to see a VA urologist. She informed me that she felt I was too young to die and she was going to have me receive one hormone treatment while they were setting up for me to have radiation treatments. I was going to have to drive one and a half hours each way for 35 days for the radiation treatments. I praying—and the members of my church were praying for me—that I would not have to do that. Sure enough to the praise of the Lord, he worked it out, and I ended up receiving the radiation treatments ten minutes from my house, and my PSA has been great ever since.

Between January 1999 and December 2008, I had a total of seven heart attacks, six stents, quadruple open heart by-pass surgery, prostate cancer surgery, and radiation treatments. During this time as a result of the extensive battery of test that were run, I discovered that I have an aorta aneurysm in my abdomen (which may require surgery), gall stones (which may require surgery), three hernias (which may require surgery), and COPD.

Over the years that I have been a Christian I have been asked to do many different jobs and things for the Lord. Any time I have been teaching, guest-speaking at a Brotherhood meeting, seniors' meeting, nursing home, county jail, Baptist Men's Day or on the few occasions I've been asked to fill in for the preacher, I have always tried to teach in one way. No matter what the scripture, lesson, or subject matter I always try to bring it out in such a manner that there is something for both the Christians & Non-Christians to learn or get from the context. A lot of people have told me that I have been such a blessing to them and that they appreciate what I do for the Lord and our church. As I have earlier mentioned I always have felt like they were the blessing to me. I would try, to the best of my ability, to teach how someone could come to know the Christ that I know or how he wanted us to live our lives.

I have tried to be an example by the way I lived my life, but I always felt that something was lacking. With the demands on my time due to the jobs I have had and running my own business I had always looked forward to the day when I would reach sixty-two and could retire. *My* plan was to then start doing something full time for the Lord. Little did I realize that God's plan for my life was completely different and that because of my health I would be on disability before my sixty-second birthday.

I have said earlier that there was a fourth thing I needed the Lord's help with but did not comprehend or understand at the time. I am not going to make any excuses, but I will try and explain the reason behind this. In 1959 I was twelve years old, and I started smoking a full pack of Camel cigarettes a day. Within a few years I was up to two packs a day and eventually two and a half packs a day. Back then there was neither the stigma nor the educational knowledge around—that there is today—regarding smoking. It was not the stupid thing but the cool thing to be doing. Again not making excuses but my Dad, whom I loved and respected, smoked all his live. After all of my heart troubles, the doctors started warning me about my smoking. I tried almost everything on the market to help me quit smoking—including private hypnotism—and nothing worked. I now realized what a true addiction was whether it be alcohol, drugs, or cigarettes. I kept telling myself that my heart problems were hereditary, for my grandfather had died in his forties from heart problems.

On April 28, 2009 I had another regular scheduled doctor's visit with my VA doctor. I got up and was getting ready to go. I was standing in front of the bathroom mirror and applied shaving cream to my face and neck and proceeded to shave. When I reached the right side of my neck, the razor went over a bump about half the size of a ping pong ball. It had not been there when I put the shaving cream on. I went on to the doctor after getting ready and he told me it could not have just popped up like that. I assured him that I knew it had.

He said in that case I had better go to my cardiologist and have them check me out, it might be an aneurysm. I started driving home and called my wife and got the phone number for my cardiologist and called his office. No one could see me that day, and they advised me to go to the emergency room. I stopped by the house, picked up Linda, and we headed to the ER. After much discussion back and forth with the hospital staff about whether this bump could have come up so fast, they decided to do a CT scan. It showed up there was something in my neck and it was not an aneurysm. The Veterans Administration scheduled me for an emergency appointment with a VA, Ear, Nose and Throat (ENT) Doctor.

It was a two hour drive from our home. When I arrived he stuck a needle in my neck and drained a lot of fluid and said it very well could have just popped up with that much fluid in it. They tested it and said they did not know what it was, but they recommended that it be removed.

May 26, 2009 I went in for surgery, and it turned out to be throat cancer which had spread to my lymph nodes in the right side of my neck. After removing five lymph nodes and the cancer from my throat, they scheduled a PET scan to insure they had gotten all the cancer. In July the scan showed there was still cancer in my throat. It was now time for a round of radiation on my neck. I had thirty-seven days of radiation and also chemotherapy. They made a mask to snap my head and neck down to a table so that I could not move during the radiation treatments, and scheduled me to have the chemo, a pick line put in my neck in order to give me the chemo, and surgery for a feeding tube to be placed in my stomach. I was going to get sick to the point I would not be able to eat and Linda would have to feed me through the tube.

Every time they would snap me down to the table, I would start praying, *Lord, I can do this with your help.*[41] Only once during the thirty-seven treatments did I holler for them to let me up. I took a couple deep breaths, said the short prayer over and over a few times, and then they snapped me back down, and I went on with the treatment with the Lord's help again.

The very first chemo treatment almost killed me. My body reacted against the treatment, and they had to stop the radiation for a week and get me back strong enough to continue the radiation. They discontinued any further chemo treatments altogether.

The first part of October, I finished the radiation treatments with almost all my taste buds being destroyed, my saliva glands shot, and unable to eat anything. I had gone from

180 lbs down to 150 lbs. Every time my wife would try and feed me through the tube, it would come up into my throat and make me sick. We tried everything, and nothing was working. Finally, on December the 23rd, I told her enough was enough—I was going to have the feeding tube removed, and I was going to learn to eat or I would just die.

Gradually I was able to eat and continued on. The place where they removed the feeding tube left an indentation in my stomach just a couple inches above my belly button and looks just like it only a little bit smaller. I told everyone at church there was some good news and some bad news about it. The bad news was that now I had two belly buttons that I had to keep lint out of. The good news was that now even the undertaker would look at me and say, he must have been born again.[42]

The first PET scan showed the cancer was gone; the next one showed it was back and about the size of a quarter in my throat and on the base of my tongue. This was late 2010.

The VA ENT was going to schedule me to have a very drastic surgery at a hospital four and a half hours from our home. They were going to cut out part of my neck and throat, take part of the inside of my left forearm and replace the hole in my neck with my forearm muscle and tissue. I told the doctor that I was not sure about that drastic of a surgery and that I was concerned with Linda having to be that far away from home. We would have to pray about it and let him know. The deductive reasoning was obvious, God would either have to miraculously heal me, or I needed to have the surgery or I would probably die from the results of the throat cancer—I would get to where I could not eat, and I was not going through the feeding tube thing again, so I would probably starve to death.

I called the doctor to see if the surgery could not be done at a hospital closer to my home and told him that I needed to discuss the surgery in more detail with the doctor who would be performing it. I live in a fairly large city with a top rated hospital, and I was unable to find any doctor who could perform this type of surgery. The VA ENT knew the head of surgery at a really large hospital in a larger city twenty miles from my house and said he would call to see if he could recommend any one. Two days later I received a phone call scheduling an appointment with an ENT who was affiliated with that hospital. It was not VA and I would have to pay the deductibles and co-pays along with my personal insurance.

It never ceases to amaze me the way the Lord works things out. The VA ENT I had been seeing had done this major surgery many times. The only reason he was not going to do it was that the VA had just stopped that facility from doing that procedure because they did not have an ENT on staff 24 hours a day, seven days a week, therefore he could not perform the procedure or surgery for that reason. The last thing he told me was that, no matter who I ended up seeing, if they were just going to take his word and his test and do the operation, to get up and leave. Any doctor who was capable of doing the surgery would want to see everything for himself.

My wife and I went to the scheduled appointment, met the new ENT that had been recommended. He started off by asking if I realized how serious and complicated of a surgery that my doctor was recommending. He went into a little detail and then proceeded to tell me that he wanted to see for himself, but that if the doctor's report and PET scan information were accurate, and the cancer was where they said and was no larger than a quarter, that he could possibly use a laser to go down my throat and burn the cancer out. What he was suggesting was that we schedule that procedure, and while he had me asleep, if he felt he could get it all out, he would go ahead with the laser surgery, if not they would wake me up, send me home and we would discuss if I wanted the other surgery scheduled at another appointment. We agreed on this plan of action, and he had to order the laser due to this being such a specialized use. We scheduled the procedure for December 10, 2010.

A very sweet lady at our church assured me that everything was going to be fine. She was over our church's Christmas play on the 19th and she wanted me at the end to give my testimony and sing *There's Something About That Name* by

Bill and Gloria Gaither. I looked at her like she was nuts and pointed out that they were going down my throat with an air tube, camera and laser to burn out part of my throat and part of the base of my tongue only nine days before the play and that they were expecting me to be in the hospital for four of those days. She told me not worry, and that she had faith. I smiled real big at her and said, "OK, we will see how it goes!"

I had the laser procedure. The doctor said everything looked good, and I came home after the scheduled four days of recovery and observation. On the 19th my wife, mother in-law, two sister-in-laws, and a brother-in-law all went to Church early to practice the last dress rehearsal before the play, making sure I was going to be okay at home and in bed. I assured them that I would be and prayed they would have a blessed program and to enjoy.

I give the Lord the Praise for what happened next. I do not remember hardly anything about it because of the pain medication they had me on, but he kept me safe. I somehow got up, dressed, drove to the church and walked in right before they were to start. I told this sweet lady that when she wanted me to testify and sing to let me know. I am told, and they have it on video tape, I went up, took the mike and proceeded to give my testimony and sing the song without a problem. My wife says there was not a dry eye in the place. Praise the Lord again.

It turned out during the next PET scan that there was still some cancer below the surface that the doctor did not see, and I had to repeat the procedure again on February 28, 2011. By this time I had gone from 150 lbs down to 130 lbs.

Another PET scan in May showed one area of just a little concern in a different part of my throat. They did another scan on September 29, 2011, and this small area had grown. I managed to get back up to 147 lbs before the next sched-uled surgery. On October 26, 2011 he performed another surgery. This time the news was not good. He could not get to all the cancer and my only alternative was to go back to the radical procedure they had first discussed, naturally with no guarantees.

I am now down to 122 lbs. It is the middle of December, and I have managed to stop losing weight. I am able to eat although with some problems and have put back on a few pounds. I have told my wife and family that this makes five times in three years that I have been to the bottom of the valley and am climbing back to the hilltop. With the Lord's help I'll make it, and as far as the remaining cancer and its growth and the speed with which it may consume me—I am leaving that entirely in the Lord's hands. I realize and accept his will in my life and that he is able to completely heal me in this body, and if not I will be healed when I receive my glorified body.[(39)] Prayerfully I'm leaving it in Jesus' hands and will continue to live one day at a time, giving the Lord the praise as long as he allows me to serve him in this earthly body. Ironically it took so much time for me to accept that he had meant for me to write this book, so much time to accept his Holy Spirit's guidance, that by the time you are reading it I might have gone on to be in his presence. [43]

Now, how this book came to be. I was ask to give my testimony at a Young at Heart luncheon for seniors, and I never pass up a chance if at all possible to witness for my Lord. You know by now that I joke and kid with people all the time, and prior to this luncheon I was in my bank and speaking with the manager, testifying to what all had happened since I had seen her last and telling her how the Lord had really blessed and been so good to me. "He sure has" she said.

As we were walking out of her office and into the lobby, I said, "The Lord still has something in mind for me, but I wish he would send me a postcard because I am getting tired of all this."

Knowing me as she does, she laughed out loud, and a man standing at the teller's position speaks up and says, "Yea, that would be nice if he did it that way."

I wanted to make sure he did not misunderstand what I was saying since he had only caught the last sentence of our conversation. I said, "It's just that I have had at least seven heart attacks, quadruple open heart surgery, two different types of cancer, four cancer surgeries, radiation treatments two different times, and one chemo treatment."

Then he said, loud enough for everyone in the bank to hear, "You are one sick S.O.B." (Though he did not use initials).

By their expressions, I think everyone around us was shocked. "No sir," I said, "you got the wrong impression, the Lord has really blessed me through it all, and I am doing great."

He quickly walked out of the bank, and the teller who'd been serving him said, "The nerve of him, it sounds to me like the Lord has really been looking after you."

The next Sunday, as I was teaching the adult men's class at our church during Sunday School, I related the story of what happened. We had some discussion about it, and I mentioned to them that sometimes I had a hard time understanding God's will in our different lives but that I could honestly say, through everything I had been through, I had never questioned God as to why this was happening to me.

A few weeks went by and it was the day of the Young at Heart Luncheon. I spoke giving my testimony for thirty minutes before lunch and sang a song. We ate, and after the lunch and during the following week, *FIVE* different people came up to me and said they wanted to hear me speak again because they could tell I was rushing my testimony, trying not to speak too long, and they wanted to hear more. They would then add, you know that you ought to write a book. I would laugh, and they would insist they were serious.

It dawned on me, as if the Lord was speaking to me, *Bill I have been telling you for thirty years I want you to write about, Believing, Salvation and Praise. I have blessed you with so much, looked after you, even sent an angel to let you know I was with you always, and you still have not obeyed me.* All of a sudden I felt like I was in the belly of a great fish. I had been steered left and right and left again over and over. I said, *Lord, you know I cannot write a book, but if that is what you want me to do, you will have to come through on that old saying—God does not necessarily call the equipped but he will equip the called.*

I have always believed strongly that all things will work out to the good.[44] I have started the writing of this book several times over the past thirty something years, but this time I knew no matter how long it took or how difficult it would be that God meant for me to set down and do it. He had sent me a postcard through five different individuals.

Over the years God has blessed me many times over. I remember Linda and I being saved from a terrible car accident where cars were slamming into one another and bouncing off the wall in the middle of the interstate—a path opened up and Linda and I drove right through without touching a single car. I remember a wreck I *was* involved in where a moped pulled out directly in front of me. Swerving hard to the left in order to miss him, I pulled directly in the path of an oncoming car with a lady and her two children; swerving again hard right I lost control of the car and ended up in a ditch totaling the restored 1973 corvette convertible the Lord had blessed me with. No one was injured, and nothing was lost but an automobile.

It is my sincere and humble prayer that I have rightly divided his word of truth.[45] That if you are a Christian these words may have been a blessing to you and might help you let your light shine brighter that others might see Christ in you; that they may uplift you in whatever circumstances you may find yourself facing in this dark world with hope and words of Praise for our Lord and Savior to glorify our Father which is in heaven. I pray that you will listen to his still small voice and not put off till tomorrow what the Lord wants you to do today. If you are a new Christian, I pray that God may give you strength and guide you in your decisions for your growth and that he will give you the peace within that you have searched for. If you have not yet received Christ, I pray that this book may be a seed that will be planted on solid ground and cause you to seek out a Bible-believing Church, with Bible-believing Teachers and Preacher and that you can come to personally know my Lord and Savior, Jesus Christ.

It has always been my desire that, when I stand before the Lord, I will have run the race in a manner that I may hear him say, *well done my good and faithful servant* and that I will have to give account for only a few bad deeds done in the body.[46] It is not as though I have done nothing for my Lord, but as I mentioned earlier I have always felt something was lacking. My genetic makeup and past experiences has always made me a Type A personality, and I have never shied away from accepting responsibility or taking charge when needed. I guess it is just that facing the real possibility that, with my throat cancer this time, it may be sooner rather than later when I will stand before him. I regret and ask his forgiveness that there may have been occasions where I went against the advice I gave you in the preceding paragraph. I may have failed to listen to his still small voice and put off till another day what he wanted me to have done yesterday.

Thought for the day!

Yours may be the very soul that the Lord has kept me alive and inspired me to write this book for. If so, he has great things in store for you. May God Bless and direct you as he has my every step along life's path. And may I continue to serve him and give him the Praise as long as he chooses for me to remain on this earth.

Until his second coming;

Our Lord's Model Prayer;

After this manner therefore pray ye: Our Father which art in heaven, Hallowed be thy name. Thy kingdom come. Thy will be done in earth, as *it is* in heaven. Give us this day our daily bread. And forgive us our debts, as we forgive our debtors. And lead us not into temptation, but deliver us from evil: For thine is the kingdom, and the power, and the glory, for ever. Amen. (Matt. 6:9–13 KJV)

"In this manner, therefore, pray: Our Father in heaven, Hallowed be Your name. Your kingdom come. Your will be done On earth as *it is* in heaven. Give us this day our daily bread. And forgive us our debts, As we forgive our debtors. And do not lead us into temptation, But deliver us from the evil one. For Yours is the kingdom and the power and the glory forever. Amen (Matt. 6:9–13 NKJV)

With a lot of books and tracts they want you to write them to let them know if you received Christ as a result of that book or tract. They have many reasons for that. Sometimes they are large organizations with the resources to send you follow-up materials to help you in your Christian walk. I am only an individual whom the Lord has blessed, and I urge you again to seek out a Bible-believing, Bible-teaching local church that can give you that support during your growth. My prayer is that if you received Christ as your personal Lord and Savior through his grace and his use of me; *PLEASE* tell a loved one, tell a friend, tell a stranger about Christ and what he has done for you, and always give the Lord the Praise, that someone else may hear and Believe, get Saved and give the Lord the Praise, and the circle will continue until his second coming!

With love in my heart, a prayer on my lips, and you on my mind,

Your Brother in Christ!

Bill Savage

ENDNOTES

1 [there is a broad and narrow way]
(1)

Enter ye in at the strait gate: for wide *is* the gate, and broad *is* the way, that leadeth to destruction, and many there be which go in thereat: Because strait *is* the gate, and narrow *is* the way, which leadeth unto life, and few there be that find it.

Beware of false prophets, which come to you in sheep's clothing, but inwardly they are ravening wolves. Ye shall know them by their fruits. Do men gather grapes of thorns, or figs of thistles? Even so every good tree bringeth forth good fruit; but a corrupt tree bringeth forth evil fruit. A good tree cannot bring forth evil fruit, neither *can* a corrupt tree bring forth good fruit. Every tree that bringeth not forth good fruit is hewn down, and cast into the fire. Wherefore by their fruits ye shall know them.

Not every one that saith unto me, Lord, Lord, shall enter into the kingdom of heaven; but he that doeth the will of my Father which is in heaven. Many will say to me in that day, Lord, Lord, have we not prophesied in thy name? and in thy name have cast out devils? and in thy name done many wonderful works? And then will I profess unto them, I never knew you: Depart from me, ye that work iniquity. (Matt. 7:13–23 KJV)

Enter by the narrow gate; for wide *is* the gate and broad *is* the way that leads to destruction, and there are many who go in by it. Because narrow *is* the gate and difficult *is* the way which leads to life, and there are few who find it.

Beware of false prophets, who come to you in sheep's clothing, but inwardly they are ravenous wolves. You will know them by their fruits. Do men gather grapes from thornbushes or figs from thistles? Even so, every good tree bears good fruit, but a bad tree bears bad fruit. A good tree cannot bear bad fruit, nor *can* a bad tree bear good fruit. Every tree that does not bear good fruit is cut down and thrown into the fire. Therefore by their fruits you will know them.

Not everyone who says to Me, 'Lord, Lord,' shall enter the kingdom of heaven, but he who does the will of My Father in heaven. Many will say to Me in that day, 'Lord, Lord, have we not prophesied in Your name, cast out demons in Your name, and done many wonders in Your name?' And then I will declare to them, 'I never knew you; depart from Me, you who practice lawlessness!' (Matt. 7:13–23 NKJV)

2   [because of the word, by and by he is offended]

Hear ye therefore the parable of the sower. When any one heareth the word of the kingdom, and understandeth *it* not, then cometh the wicked *one*, and catcheth away that which was sown in his heart. This is he which received seed by the way side. But he that received the seed into stony places, the same is he that heareth the word, and anon with joy receiveth it; Yet hath he not root in himself, but dureth for a while: for when tribulation or persecution ariseth because of the word, by and by he is offended. He also that received seed among the thorns is he that heareth the word; and the care of this world, and the deceitfulness of riches, choke the word, and he becometh unfruitful. **But he that received seed into the good ground is he that heareth the word, and understandeth *it*; which also beareth fruit, and bringeth forth, some an hundredfold, some sixty, some thirty.** (Matt. 13:18–23 KJV)

Therefore hear the parable of the sower: When anyone hears the word of the kingdom, and does not understand *it*, then the wicked *one* comes and snatches away what was sown in his heart. This is he who received seed by the wayside. But he who received the seed on stony places, this is he who hears the word and immediately receives it with joy; yet he has no root in himself, but endures only for a while. For when tribulation or persecution arises because of the word, immediately he stumbles. Now he who received seed among the thorns is he who hears the word, and the cares of this world and the deceitfulness of riches choke the word, and he becomes unfruitful. But he who received seed on the good ground is he who hears the word and understands *it*, who indeed bears fruit and produces: some a hundredfold, some sixty, some thirty. (Matt. 13:18–23 NKJV)

3   [Ye men of Athens...]

Then Paul stood in the midst of Mars' hill, and said, *Ye* men of Athens, I perceive that in all things ye are too superstitious. For as I passed by, and beheld your devotions, I found an altar with this inscription, TO THE UNKNOWN GOD. Whom therefore ye ignorantly worship, him declare I unto you. God that made the world and all things therein, seeing that he is Lord of heaven and earth, dwelleth not in temples made with hands; Neither is worshipped with men's hands, as though he needed any thing, seeing he giveth to all life, and breath, and all things; And hath made of one blood all nations of men for to dwell on all the face of the earth, and hath determined the times before appointed, and the bounds of their habitation; That they should seek the Lord, if haply they might feel after him, and find him, though he be not far from every one of us: For in him we live, and move, and have our being; as certain also of your own poets have said, For we are also his offspring. Forasmuch then as we are the offspring of God, we ought not to think that the Godhead is like unto gold, or silver, or stone, graven by art and man's device. And the times of this ignorance God winked at; but now commandeth all men every where to repent: Because he hath appointed a day, in the which he will judge the world in righteousness by *that* man whom he hath ordained; *whereof* he hath given assurance unto all *men*, in that he hath raised him from the dead. (Acts 17:22–31 KJV)

Then Paul stood in the midst of the Areopagus and said, "Men of Athens, I perceive that in all things you are very religious; for as I was passing through and considering the objects of your worship, I even found an altar with this inscription: TO THE UNKNOWN GOD. Therefore, the One whom you worship without knowing, Him I proclaim to you: God, who made the world and everything in it, since He is Lord of heaven and earth, does not dwell in temples made with hands. Nor is He worshiped with men's hands, as though He needed anything, since He gives to all life, breath, and all things. And He has made from one blood every nation of men to dwell on all the face of the earth, and has determined their preappointed times and the boundaries of their dwellings, so that they should seek the Lord, in the hope that they might grope for Him and find Him, though He is not far from each one of us; for in Him we live and move and have our being, as also some of your own poets have said, 'For we are also His offspring.' Therefore, since we are the offspring of God, we ought not to think that the Divine Nature is like gold or silver or stone, something shaped by art and man's devising. Truly, these times of ignorance God overlooked, but now commands all men everywhere to repent, because He has appointed a day on which He will judge the world in righteousness by the Man whom He has ordained. He has given assurance of this to all by raising Him from the dead." (Acts 17:22–31 NKJV)

4   [All our righteousnesses...]

But we are all as an unclean *thing*, and all our righteousnesses *are* as filthy rags; and we all do fade as a leaf; and our iniquities, like the wind, have taken us away. (Isa. 64:6 KJV)

But we are all like an unclean *thing*, And all our righteousnesses *are* like filthy rags; We all fade as a leaf, And our iniquities, like the wind, Have taken us away. (Isa. 64:6 NKJV)

5   [...These are the words which I spake...]

And as they thus spake, Jesus himself stood in the midst of them, and saith unto them, **Peace *be* unto you.** But they were terrified and affrighted, and supposed that they had seen a spirit. And he said unto them, **Why are ye troubled? and why do thoughts arise in your hearts? Behold my hands and my feet, that it is I myself: handle me, and see; for a spirit hath not flesh and bones, as ye see me have.** And when he had thus spoken, he shewed them *his* hands and *his* feet. And while they yet believed not for joy, and wondered, he said unto them, **Have ye here any meat?** And they gave him a piece of a broiled fish, and of an honeycomb. And he took *it*, and did eat before them. And he said unto them, **These *are* the words which I spake unto you, while I was yet with you, that all things must be fulfilled, which were written in the law of Moses, and *in* the prophets, and *in* the psalms, concerning me.** Then opened he their understanding, that they might understand the scriptures, And said unto them, **Thus it is written, and thus it behoved Christ to suffer, and to rise from the dead the third day: And that repentance and remission of sins should be preached in his name among all nations, beginning at Jerusalem. And ye are witnesses of these things.**

And, behold, I send the promise of my Father upon you: but tarry ye in the city of Jerusalem, until ye be endued with power from on high. And he led them out as far as to Bethany, and he lifted up his hands, and blessed them. And it came to pass, while he blessed them, he was parted from them, and carried up into heaven. And they worshipped him, and returned to Jerusalem with great joy: And were continually in the temple, praising and blessing God. Amen. (Luke 24:36–53 KJV)

Now as they said these things, Jesus Himself stood in the midst of them, and said to them, **"Peace to you."** But they were terrified and frightened, and supposed they had seen a spirit. And He said to them, **"Why are you troubled? And why do doubts arise in your hearts? Behold My hands and My feet, that it is I Myself. Handle Me and see, for a spirit does not have flesh and bones as you see I have."** When He had said this, He showed them His hands and His feet. But while they still did not believe for joy, and marveled, He said to them, **"Have you any food here?"** So they gave Him a piece of a broiled fish and some honeycomb. And He took *it* and ate in their presence. Then He said to them, **"These *are* the words which I spoke to you while I was still with you, that all things must be fulfilled which were written in the Law of Moses and *the* Prophets and *the* Psalms concerning Me."** And He opened their understanding, that they might comprehend the Scriptures. Then He said to them, **"Thus it is written, and thus it was necessary for the Christ to suffer and to rise from the dead the third day, and that repentance and remission of sins should be preached in His name to all nations, beginning at Jerusalem. And you are witnesses of these things.**

"Behold, I send the Promise of My Father upon you; but tarry in the city of Jerusalem until you are endued with power from on high." And He led them out as far as Bethany, and He lifted up His hands and blessed them. Now it came to pass, while He blessed them, that He was parted from them and carried up into heaven. And they worshiped Him, and returned to Jerusalem with great joy, and were continually in the temple praising and blessing God. Amen. (Luke 24:36–53 NKJV)

6   [Thou art the Christ, the Son of the living God.]

When Jesus came into the coasts of Caesarea Philippi, he asked his disciples, saying, **Whom do men say that I the Son of man am?** And they said, Some *say that thou art* John the Baptist: some, Elias; and others, Jeremias, or one of the prophets. He saith unto them, **But whom say ye that I am?** And Simon Peter answered and said, Thou art the Christ, the Son of the living God. And Jesus answered and said unto him, **Blessed art thou, Simon Barjona: for flesh and blood hath not revealed it unto thee, but my Father which is in heaven.** (Matt. 16:13–17 KJV)

When Jesus came into the region of Caesarea Philippi, He asked His disciples, saying, **"Who do men say that I, the Son of Man, am?"** So they said, "Some *say* John the Baptist, some Elijah, and others Jeremiah or one of the prophets." He said to them, **"But who do you say that I am?"** Simon Peter answered and said, "You are the Christ, the Son of the living God." Jesus answered and said to him, **"Blessed are you, Simon Bar-Jonah, for flesh and blood has not revealed *this* to you, but My Father who is in heaven."** (Matt. 16:13–17 NKJV)

7   [Except I shall see in his hands...]

But Thomas, one of the twelve, called Didymus, was not with them when Jesus came. The other disciples therefore said unto him, We have seen the Lord. But he said unto them, Except I shall see in his hands the print of the nails, and put my finger into the print of the nails, and thrust my hand into his side, I will not believe.

And after eight days again his disciples were within, and Thomas with them: *then* came Jesus, the doors being shut, and stood in the midst, and said, **Peace *be* unto you.** Then saith he to Thomas, **Reach hither thy finger, and behold my hands; and reach hither thy hand, and thrust *it* into**

my side: and be not faithless, but believing. And Thomas answered and said unto him, My Lord and my God. Jesus saith unto him, **Thomas, because thou hast seen me, thou hast believed: blessed *are* they that have not seen, and *yet* have believed.** (John 20:24–29 KJV)

Now Thomas, called the Twin, one of the twelve, was not with them when Jesus came. The other disciples therefore said to him, "We have seen the Lord." So he said to them, "Unless I see in His hands the print of the nails, and put my finger into the print of the nails, and put my hand into His side, I will not believe."

And after eight days His disciples were again inside, and Thomas with them. Jesus came, the doors being shut, and stood in the midst, and said, **"Peace to you!"** Then He said to Thomas, **"Reach your finger here, and look at My hands; and reach your hand *here*, and put *it* into My side. Do not be unbelieving, but believing."** And Thomas answered and said to Him, "My Lord and my God!" Jesus said to him, **"Thomas, because you have seen Me, you have believed. Blessed *are* those who have not seen and *yet* have believed."** (John 20:24–29 NKJV)

<u>8</u>   [But we are all as an unclean thing...]

But we are all as an unclean *thing*, and all our righteousnesses *are* as filthy rags; and we all do fade as a leaf; and our iniquities, like the wind, have taken us away. And *there* is none that calleth upon thy name, that stirreth up himself to take hold of thee: for thou hast hid thy face from us, and hast consumed us, because of our iniquities. But now, O LORD, thou *art* our father; we *are* the clay, and thou our potter; and we all *are* the work of thy hand. (Isa. 64:6–8 KJV)

But we are all like an unclean *thing*, And all our righteousnesses *are* like filthy rags; We all fade as a leaf, And our iniquities, like the wind, Have taken us away. And *there is* no one who calls on Your name, Who stirs himself up to take hold of You; For You have hidden Your face from us, And have consumed us because of our iniquities. But now, O LORD, You *are* our Father; We *are* the clay, and You our potter; And all we *are* the work of Your hand. (Isa. 64:6–8 NKJV)

9   [The Second Death]

And death and hell were cast into the lake of fire. This is the second death. (Rev. 20:14 KJV)

But the fearful, and unbelieving, and the abominable, and murderers, and whoremongers, and sorcerers, and idolaters, and all liars, shall have their part in the lake which burneth with fire and brimstone: which is the second death. (Rev. 21:8 KJV)

Then Death and Hades were cast into the lake of fire. This is the second death. (Rev. 20:14 NKJV)

"But the cowardly, unbelieving, abominable, murderers, sexually immoral, sorcerers, idolaters, and all liars shall have their part in the lake which burns with fire and brimstone, which is the second death." (Rev. 21:8 NKJV)

10   [Picture the running water as God]

Jesus answered and said unto her, **If thou knewest the gift of God, and who it is that saith to thee, Give me to drink; thou wouldest have asked of him, and he would have given thee living water.** (John 4:10 KJV)

And I saw a new heaven and a new earth: for the first heaven and the first earth were passed away; and there was no more sea. And I John saw the holy city, new Jerusalem, coming down from God out of heaven, prepared as a bride adorned for her husband. And I heard a great voice out of heaven saying, Behold, the tabernacle of God *is* with men, and he will dwell with them, and they shall be his people, and God himself shall be with them, *and be* their God. And God shall wipe away all tears from their eyes; and there shall be no more death, neither sorrow, nor crying, neither shall there be any more pain: for the former things are passed away. And he that sat upon the throne said, Behold, I make all things new. And he said unto me, Write: for these words are true and faithful. And he said unto me, It is done. I am Alpha and Omega, the beginning and the end. I will give unto him that is athirst of the fountain of the water of life freely. He that overcometh shall inherit all things; and I will be his God, and he shall be my son. But the fearful, and unbelieving, and the abominable, and murderers, and whoremongers, and sorcerers, and idolaters, and all liars, shall have their part in the lake which burneth with fire and brimstone: which is the second death. (Rev. 21:1–8 KJV)

Jesus answered and said to her, **"If you knew the gift of God, and who it is who says to you, 'Give Me a drink,' you would have asked Him, and He would have given you living water."** (John 4:10 NKJV)

Now I saw a new heaven and a new earth, for the first heaven and the first earth had passed away. Also there was no more sea. Then I, John, saw the holy city, New Jerusalem, coming down out of heaven from God, prepared as a bride adorned for her husband. And I heard a loud voice from heaven saying, "Behold, the tabernacle of God *is* with men, and He will dwell with them, and they shall be His people. God Himself will be with them *and be* their God. And God will wipe away every tear from their eyes; there shall be no more death, nor sorrow, nor crying. There shall be no more pain, for the former things have passed away." Then He who sat on the throne said, "Behold, I make all things new." And He said to me, "Write, for these words are true and faithful." And He said to me, "It is done! I am the Alpha and the Omega, the Beginning and the End. I will give of the fountain of the water of life freely to him who thirsts. He who overcomes shall inherit all things, and I will be his God and he shall be My son. But the cowardly, unbelieving, abominable, murderers, sexually immoral, sorcerers, idolaters, and all liars shall have their part in the lake which burns with fire and brimstone, which is the second death." (Rev. 21:1–8 NKJV)

11 [The power plant and power lines are the
Holy Spirit]

(11)

In the last day, that great *day* of the feast, Jesus stood and cried, saying, **If any man thirst, let him come unto me, and drink. He that believeth on me, as the scripture hath said, out of his belly shall flow rivers of living water.** (But this spake he of the Spirit, which they that believe on him should receive: for the Holy Ghost was not yet *given*; because that Jesus was not yet glorified.) (John 7:37–39 KJV)

And I will pray the Father, and he shall give you another Comforter, that he may abide with you for ever; *Even* **the Spirit of truth; whom the world cannot receive, because it seeth him not, neither knoweth him: but ye know him; for he dwelleth with you, and shall be in you. I will not leave you comfortless: I will come to you. Yet a little while, and the world seeth me no more; but ye see me: because I live, ye shall live also. At that day ye shall know that I** *am* **in my Father, and ye in me, and I in you.** (John 14:16–20 KJV)

On the last day, that great *day* of the feast, Jesus stood and cried out, saying, **"If anyone thirsts, let him come to Me and drink. He who believes in Me, as the Scripture has said, out of his heart will flow rivers of living water."** But this He spoke concerning the Spirit, whom those believing in Him would receive; for the Holy Spirit was not yet *given*, because Jesus was not yet glorified. (John 7:37–39 NKJV)

"And I will pray the Father, and He will give you another Helper, that He may abide with you forever—the Spirit of truth, whom the world cannot receive, because it neither sees Him nor knows Him; but you know Him, for He dwells with you and will be in you. I will not leave you orphans; I will come to you. A little while longer and the world will see Me no more, but you will see Me. Because I live, you will live also. At that day you will know that I *am* **in My Father, and you in Me, and I in you."** (John 14:16–20 NKJV)

12   [The light switch on the wall is our brains
      or mind and the light is our hearts]
(12)

**Ye are the light of the world. A city that is set on an hill
cannot be hid. Neither do men light a candle, and put
it under a bushel, but on a candlestick; and it giveth
light unto all that are in the house. Let your light so
shine before men, that they may see your good works,
and glorify your Father which is in heaven.** (Matt.
5:14–16 KJV)

But if our gospel be hid, it is hid to them that are lost: In
whom the god of this world hath blinded the minds of them
which believe not, lest the light of the glorious gospel of
Christ, who is the image of God, should shine unto them. For
we preach not ourselves, but Christ Jesus the Lord; and
ourselves your servants for Jesus' sake. For God, who commanded the light to shine out of darkness, hath shined in our
hearts, to *give* the light of the knowledge of the glory of God
in the face of Jesus Christ. (2 Cor. 4:3–6 KJV)

**"You are the light of the world. A city that is set on a hill
cannot be hidden. Nor do they light a lamp and put it
under a basket, but on a lampstand, and it gives light to
all *who are* in the house. Let your light so shine before
men, that they may see your good works and glorify
your Father in heaven."** (Matt. 5:14–16 NKJV)

But even if our gospel is veiled, it is veiled to those who
are perishing, whose minds the god of this age has blinded,
who do not believe, lest the light of the gospel of the glory
of Christ, who is the image of God, should shine on them.
For we do not preach ourselves, but Christ Jesus the Lord,
and ourselves your bondservants for Jesus' sake. For it is
the God who commanded light to shine out of darkness,
who has shone in our hearts to *give* the light of the knowledge of the glory of God in the face of Jesus Christ. (2 Cor.
4:3–6 NKJV)

13   [God's free gift]
(13)   ((13))

For by grace are ye saved through faith; and that not of yourselves: *it is* the gift of God: Not of works, lest any man should boast. (Eph. 2:8–9 KJV)

For by grace you have been saved through faith, and that not of yourselves; *it is* the gift of God, not of works, lest anyone should boast. (Eph. 2:8–9 NKJV)

14   [God took away my heart of stone]

And I will give them one heart, and I will put a new spirit within you; and I will take the stony heart out of their flesh, and will give them an heart of flesh: That they may walk in my statutes, and keep mine ordinances, and do them: and they shall be my people, and I will be their God. (Ezek. 11:19–20 KJV)

Therefore if any man *be* in Christ, *he is* a new creature: old things are passed away; behold, all things are become new. (2 Cor. 5:17 KJV)

As far as the east is from the west, *so* far hath he removed our transgressions from us. (Ps. 103:12 KJV)

"Then I will give them one heart, and I will put a new spirit within them, and take the stony heart out of their flesh, and give them a heart of flesh, that they may walk in My statutes and keep My judgments and do them; and they shall be My people, and I will be their God." (Ezek. 11:19–20 NKJV)

Therefore, if anyone *is* in Christ, *he is* a new creation; old things have passed away; behold, all things have become new. (2 Cor. 5:17 NKJV)

As far as the east is from the west, *So* far has He removed our transgressions from us. (Ps. 103:12 NKJV)

15 [if I could understand the Bible then maybe I could believe it]
(15)

Which things also we speak, not in the words which man's wisdom teacheth, but which the Holy Ghost teacheth; comparing spiritual things with spiritual. (1 Cor. 2:13 KJV)

These things we also speak, not in words which man's wisdom teaches but which the Holy Spirit teaches, comparing spiritual things with spiritual. (1 Cor. 2:13 NKJV)

16 [When you accept that the intelligent designer]

Genesis Chapter 1, KJV

Creation of heaven and earth

In the beginning God created the heaven and the earth. And the earth was without form, and void; and darkness *was* upon the face of the deep. And the Spirit of God moved upon the face of the waters.

Creation of the light

And God said, Let there be light: and there was light. And God saw the light, that *it was* good: and God divided the light from the darkness. And God called the light Day, and the darkness he called Night. And the evening and the morning were the first day.

Creation of the firmament

And God said, Let there be a firmament in the midst of the waters, and let it divide the waters from the waters. And God made the firmament, and divided the waters which *were* under the firmament from the waters which *were* above the firmament: and it was so. And God called the firmament Heaven. And the evening and the morning were the second day.

The earth separated from the waters

And God said, Let the waters under the heaven be gathered together unto one place, and let the dry *land* appear: and it was so. And God called the dry *land* Earth; and the gathering together of the waters called he Seas: and God saw that *it was* good. And God said, Let the earth bring forth grass, the herb yielding seed, *and* the fruit tree yielding fruit after his kind, whose seed *is* in itself, upon the earth: and it was so. And the earth brought forth grass, *and* herb yielding seed after his kind, and the tree yielding fruit, whose seed *was* in itself, after his kind: and God saw that *it was* good. And the evening and the morning were the third day.

Creation of the sun, moon and stars

And God said, Let there be lights in the firmament of the heaven to divide the day from the night; and let them be for signs, and for seasons, and for days, and years: And let them be for lights in the firmament of the heaven to give light upon the earth: and it was so. And God made two great lights; the greater light to rule the day, and the lesser light to rule the night: *he made* the stars also. And God set them in the firmament of the heaven to give light upon the earth, And to rule over the day and over the night, and to divide the light from the darkness: and God saw that *it was* good. And the evening and the morning were the fourth day.

Creation of fish, fowl, beasts and cattle

And God said, Let the waters bring forth abundantly the moving creature that hath life, and fowl *that* may fly above the earth in the open firmament of heaven. And God created great whales, and every living creature that moveth, which the waters brought forth abundantly, after their kind, and every winged fowl after his kind: and God saw that *it was* good. And God blessed them, saying, Be fruitful, and multiply, and fill the waters in the seas, and let fowl multiply in the earth. And the evening and the morning were the fifth day. And God said, Let the earth bring forth the living creature after his kind, cattle, and creeping thing, and beast of the earth after his kind: and it was so. And God made the beast of the earth after his kind, and cattle after their kind, and every thing that creepeth upon the earth after his kind: and God saw that *it was* good.

Creation man in the image of God

And God said, Let us make man in our image, after our likeness: and let them have dominion over the fish of the sea, and over the fowl of the air, and over the cattle, and over all the earth, and over every creeping thing that creepeth upon the earth. So God created man in his *own* image, in the image of God created he him; male and female created he them. And God blessed them, and God said unto them, Be fruitful, and multiply, and replenish the earth, and subdue it: and have dominion over the fish of the sea, and over the fowl of the air, and over every living thing that moveth upon the earth.

Provision for food

And God said, Behold, I have given you every herb bearing seed, which *is* upon the face of all the earth, and every tree, in the which *is* the fruit of a tree yielding seed; to you it shall be for meat. And to every beast of the earth, and to every fowl of the air, and to every thing that creepeth upon the earth, wherein *there is* life, *I have given* every green herb for meat: and it was so. And God saw every thing that he had made, and, behold, *it was* very good. And the evening and the morning were the sixth day.

Genesis Chapter 2, KJV

The first Sabbath

Thus the heavens and the earth were finished, and all the host of them. And on the seventh day God ended his work which he had made; and he rested on the seventh day from all his work which he had made. And God blessed the seventh day, and sanctified it: because that in it he had rested from all his work which God created and made.

The manner of the creation

These *are* the generations of the heavens and of the earth when they were created, in the day that the LORD God made the earth and the heavens, And every plant of the field before it was in the earth, and every herb of the field before it grew: for the LORD God had not caused it to rain upon the earth, and *there was* not a man to till the ground. But there went up a mist from the earth, and watered the whole face of the ground. And the LORD God formed man *of* the dust of the ground, and breathed into his nostrils the breath of life; and man became a living soul.

The garden of Eden, and the river thereof

And the LORD God planted a garden eastward in Eden; and there he put the man whom he had formed. And out of the ground made the LORD God to grow every tree that is pleasant to the sight, and good for food; the tree of life also in the midst of the garden, and the tree of knowledge of good and evil. And a river went out of Eden to water the garden; and from thence it was parted, and became into four heads. The name of the first *is* Pison: that *is* it which compasseth the whole land of Havilah, where *there is* gold; And the gold of that land *is* good: there *is* bdellium and the onyx stone. And the name of the second river *is* Gihon: the same *is* it that compasseth the whole land of Ethiopia. And the name of the third river *is* Hiddekel: that *is* it which goeth toward the east of Assyria. And the fourth river *is* Euphrates. And the LORD God took the man, and put him into the garden of Eden to dress it and to keep it. And the LORD God commanded the man, saying, Of every tree of the garden thou mayest freely eat: But of the tree of the knowledge of good and evil, thou shalt not eat of it: for in the day that thou eatest thereof thou shalt surely die.

And the LORD God said, *It is* not good that the man should be alone; I will make him an help meet for him. And out of the ground the LORD God formed every beast of the field, and every fowl of the air; and brought *them* unto Adam to see what he would call them: and whatsoever Adam called every living creature, that *was* the name thereof. And Adam gave names to all cattle, and to the fowl of the air, and to every beast of the field; but for Adam there was not found an help meet for him.

The making of woman and the institution of marriage

And the LORD God caused a deep sleep to fall upon Adam, and he slept: and he took one of his ribs, and closed up the flesh instead thereof; And the rib, which the LORD God had taken from man, made he a woman, and brought her unto the man. And Adam said, This *is* now bone of my bones, and flesh of my flesh: she shall be called Woman, because she was taken out of Man. Therefore shall a man leave his father and his mother, and shall cleave unto his wife: and they shall be one flesh. And they were both naked, the man and his wife, and were not ashamed.

Genesis Chapter 3, KJV

The serpent's deception and man's shameful fall

Now the serpent was more subtil than any beast of the field which the LORD God had made. And he said unto the woman, Yea, hath God said, Ye shall not eat of every tree of the garden?

And the woman said unto the serpent, We may eat of the fruit of the trees of the garden: But of the fruit of the tree which *is* in the midst of the garden, God hath said, Ye shall not eat of it, neither shall ye touch it, lest ye die. And the serpent said unto the woman, Ye shall not surely die: For God doth know that in the day ye eat thereof, then your eyes shall be opened, and ye shall be as gods, knowing good and evil. And when the woman saw that the tree *wa*s good for food, and that it *was* pleasant to the eyes, and a tree to be desired to make *one* wise, she took of the fruit thereof, and did eat, and gave also unto her husband with her; and he did eat. And the eyes of them both were opened, and they knew that they *were* naked; and they sewed fig leaves together, and made themselves aprons. And they heard the voice of the LORD God walking in the garden in the cool of the day: and Adam and his wife hid themselves from the presence of the LORD God amongst the trees of the garden.

God arraigns Adam and Eve

And the LORD God called unto Adam, and said unto him, Where *art* thou? And he said, I heard thy voice in the garden, and I was afraid, because I *was* naked; and I hid myself. And he said, Who told thee that thou *wast* naked? Hast thou eaten of the tree, whereof I commanded thee that thou shouldest not eat? And the man said, The woman whom thou gavest *to be* with me, she gave me of the tree, and I did eat. And the LORD God said unto the woman, What *is* this *that* thou hast done? And the woman said, The serpent beguiled me, and I did eat.

The serpent is cursed above all beasts

And the LORD God said unto the serpent, Because thou hast done this, thou *art* cursed above all cattle, and above every beast of the field; upon thy belly shalt thou go, and dust shalt thou eat all the days of thy life: And I will put enmity between thee and the woman, and between thy seed and her seed; it shall bruise thy head, and thou shalt bruise his heel.

The punishment God promises for mankind

Unto the woman he said, I will greatly multiply thy sorrow and thy conception; in sorrow thou shalt bring forth children; and thy desire *shall be* to thy husband, and he shall rule over thee. And unto Adam he said, Because thou hast hearkened unto the voice of thy wife, and hast eaten of the tree, of which I commanded thee, saying, Thou shalt not eat of it: cursed *is* the ground for thy sake; in sorrow shalt thou eat *of* it all the days of thy life; Thorns also and thistles shall it bring forth to thee; and thou shalt eat the herb of the field; In the sweat of thy face shalt thou eat bread, till thou return unto the ground; for out of it wast thou taken: for dust thou *art*, and unto dust shalt thou return. And Adam called his wife's name Eve; because she was the mother of all living. Unto Adam also and to his wife did the LORD God make coats of skins, and clothed them. And the LORD God said, Behold, the man is become as one of us, to know good and evil: and now, lest he put forth his hand, and take also of the tree of life, and eat, and live for ever: Therefore the LORD God sent him forth from the garden of Eden, to till the ground from whence he was taken. So he drove out the man; and he placed at the east of the garden of Eden Cherubims, and a flaming sword which turned every way, to keep the way of the tree of life.

16

Genesis Chapter 1, NKJV

The History of Creation

In the beginning God created the heavens and the earth. The earth was without form, and void; and darkness *was* on the face of the deep. And the Spirit of God was hovering over the face of the waters.

Then God said, "Let there be light"; and there was light. And God saw the light, that *it was* good; and God divided the light from the darkness. God called the light Day, and the darkness He called Night. So the evening and the morning were the first day.

Then God said, "Let there be a firmament in the midst of the waters, and let it divide the waters from the waters." Thus God made the firmament, and divided the waters which *were* under the firmament from the waters which *were* above the firmament; and it was so. And God called the firmament Heaven. So the evening and the morning were the second day.

Then God said, "Let the waters under the heavens be gathered together into one place, and let the dry *land* appear"; and it was so. And God called the dry *land* Earth, and the gathering together of the waters He called Seas. And God saw that *it was* good. Then God said, "Let the earth bring forth grass, the herb *that* yields seed, *and* the fruit tree *that* yields fruit according to its kind, whose seed *is* in itself, on the earth"; and it was so. And the earth brought forth grass, the herb *tha*t yields seed according to its kind, and the tree *that* yields fruit, whose seed *is* in itself according to its kind. And God saw that *it was* good. So the evening and the morning were the third day.

Then God said, "Let there be lights in the firmament of the heavens to divide the day from the night; and let them be for signs and seasons, and for days and years; and let them be for lights in the firmament of the heavens to give light on the earth"; and it was so. Then God made two great lights: the greater light to rule the day, and the lesser light to rule the night. *He made* the stars also. God set them in the firmament of the heavens to give light on the earth, and to rule over the day and over the night, and to divide the light from the darkness. And God saw that *it was* good. So the evening and the morning were the fourth day. Then God said, "Let the waters abound with an abundance of living creatures, and let birds fly above the earth across the face of the firmament of the heavens." So God created great sea creatures and every living thing that moves, with which the waters abounded, according to their kind, and every winged bird according to its kind. And God saw that *it was* good. And God blessed them, saying, "Be fruitful and multiply, and fill the waters in the seas, and let birds multiply on the earth." So the evening and the morning were the fifth day.

Then God said, "Let the earth bring forth the living creature according to its kind: cattle and creeping thing and beast of the earth, *each* according to its kind"; and it was so. And God made the beast of the earth according to its kind, cattle according to its kind, and everything that creeps on the earth according to its kind. And God saw that *it was* good.

Then God said, "Let Us make man in Our image, according to Our likeness; let them have dominion over the fish of the sea, over the birds of the air, and over the cattle, over all the earth and over every creeping thing that creeps on the earth." So God created man in His *own* image; in the image of God He created him; male and female He created them. Then God blessed them, and God said to them, "Be fruitful and multiply; fill the earth and subdue it; have dominion over the fish of the sea, over the birds of the air, and over every living thing that moves on the earth."

And God said, "See, I have given you every herb *that* yields seed which *is* on the face of all the earth, and every tree whose fruit yields seed; to you it shall be for food. Also, to every beast of the earth, to every bird of the air, and to everything that creeps on the earth, in which *there is* life, *I have given* every green herb for food"; and it was so. Then God saw everything that He had made, and indeed *it was* very good. So the evening and the morning were the sixth day.

Genesis Chapter 2, NKJV

Thus the heavens and the earth, and all the host of them, were finished. And on the seventh day God ended His work which He had done, and He rested on the seventh day from all His work which He had done. Then God blessed the seventh day and sanctified it, because in it He rested from all His work which God had created and made.

This *is* the history of the heavens and the earth when they were created, in the day that the LORD God made the earth and the heavens, before any plant of the field was in the earth and before any herb of the field had grown. For the LORD God had not caused it to rain on the earth, and *there was* no man to till the ground; but a mist went up from the earth and watered the whole face of the ground. And the LORD God formed man *of* the dust of the ground, and breathed into his nostrils the breath of life; and man became a living being.

Life in God's Garden

The LORD God planted a garden eastward in Eden, and there He put the man whom He had formed. And out of the ground the LORD God made every tree grow that is pleasant to the sight and good for food. The tree of life *was* also in the midst of the garden, and the tree of the knowledge of good and evil. Now a river went out of Eden to water the garden, and from there it parted and became four riverheads. The name of the first *is* Pishon; it *is* the one which skirts the whole land of Havilah, where *there is* gold. And the gold of that land *is* good. Bdellium and the onyx stone *are* there. The name of the second river *is* Gihon; it *is* the one which goes around the whole land of Cush. The name of the third river *is* Hiddekel; it *is* the one which goes toward the east of Assyria. The fourth river *is* the Euphrates. Then the LORD God took the man and put him in the garden of Eden to tend and keep it. And the LORD God commanded the man, saying, "Of every tree of the garden you may freely eat; but of the tree of the knowledge of good and evil you shall not eat, for in the day that you eat of it you shall surely die."

And the LORD God said, "*It is* not good that man should be alone; I will make him a helper comparable to him." Out of the ground the LORD God formed every beast of the field and every bird of the air, and brought *them* to Adam to see what he would call them. And whatever Adam called each living creature, that *was* its name. So Adam gave names to all cattle, to the birds of the air, and to every beast of the field. But for Adam there was not found a helper comparable to him. And the LORD God caused a deep sleep to fall on Adam, and he slept; and He took one of his ribs, and closed up the flesh in its place. Then the rib which the LORD God had taken from man He made into a woman, and He brought her to the man. And Adam said: "This *is* now bone of my bones And flesh of my flesh; She shall be called Woman, Because she was taken out of Man." Therefore a man shall leave his father and mother and be joined to his wife, and they shall become one flesh. And they were both naked, the man and his wife, and were not ashamed.

Genesis Chapter 3, NKJV

The Temptation and Fall of Man

Now the serpent was more cunning than any beast of the field which the LORD God had made. And he said to the woman, "Has God indeed said, 'You shall not eat of every tree of the garden'?"

And the woman said to the serpent, "We may eat the fruit of the trees of the garden; but of the fruit of the tree which *is* in the midst of the garden, God has said, 'You shall not eat it, nor shall you touch it, lest you die.'" Then the serpent said to the woman, "You will not surely die. For God knows that in the day you eat of it your eyes will be opened, and you will be like God, knowing good and evil." So when the woman saw that the tree *was* good for food, that it *was* pleasant to the eyes, and a tree desirable to make *one* wise, she took of its fruit and ate. She also gave to her husband with her, and he ate. Then the eyes of both of them were opened, and they knew that they *were* naked; and they sewed fig leaves together and made themselves coverings. And they heard the sound of the LORD God walking in the garden in the cool of the day, and Adam and his wife hid themselves from the presence of the LORD God among the trees of the garden. Then the LORD God called to Adam and said to him, "Where *are* you?" So he said, "I heard Your voice in the garden, and I was afraid because I was naked; and I hid myself." And He said, "Who told you that you *were* naked? Have you eaten from the tree of which I commanded you that you should not eat?" Then the man said, "The woman whom You gave *to be* with me, she gave me of the tree, and I ate." And the LORD God said to the woman, "What *is* this you have done?" The woman said, "The serpent deceived me, and I ate." So the LORD God said to the serpent: "Because you have done this, You *are* cursed more than all cattle, And more than every beast of the field; On your belly you shall go, And you shall eat dust All the days of your life. And I will put enmity Between you and the woman, And between your seed and her Seed; He shall bruise your head, And you shall bruise His heel." To the woman He said: "I will greatly multiply your sorrow and your conception; In pain you shall bring forth children; Your desire *shall be* for your husband, And he shall rule over you." Then to Adam He said, "Because you have heeded the voice of your wife, and have eaten from the tree of which I commanded you, saying, 'You shall not eat of it': Cursed *is* the ground for your sake; In toil you shall eat *of* it All the days of your life. Both thorns and thistles it shall bring forth for you, And you shall eat the herb of the field. In the sweat of your face you shall eat bread Till you return to the ground, For out of it you were taken; For dust you *are*, And to dust you shall return." And Adam called his wife's name Eve, because she was the mother of all living. Also for Adam and his wife the LORD God made tunics of skin, and clothed them. Then the

LORD God said, "Behold, the man has become like one of Us, to know good and evil. And now, lest he put out his hand and take also of the tree of life, and eat, and live forever"— therefore the LORD God sent him out of the garden of Eden to till the ground from which he was taken. So He drove out the man; and He placed cherubim at the east of the garden of Eden, and a flaming sword which turned every way, to guard the way to the tree of life.
16

17 [sacrificed for your sins]

And as it is appointed unto men once to die, but after this the judgment: So Christ was once offered to bear the sins of many; and unto them that look for him shall he appear the second time without sin unto salvation. (Heb. 9:27–28 KJV)

And as it is appointed for men to die once, but after this the judgment, so Christ was offered once to bear the sins of many. To those who eagerly wait for Him He will appear a second time, apart from sin, for salvation. (Heb. 9:27–28 NKJV)

18 [I came not to call the righteous]

When Jesus heard *it*, he saith unto them, **They that are whole have no need of the physician, but they that are sick: I came not to call the righteous, but sinners to repentance.** (Mark 2:17 KJV)

When Jesus heard *it*, He said to them, **"Those who are well have no need of a physician, but those who are sick. I did not come to call *the* righteous, but sinners, to repentance."** (Mark 2:17 NKJV)

19   [over one sinner that repenteth]

I say unto you, that likewise joy shall be in heaven over one sinner that repenteth, more than over ninety and nine just persons, which need no repentance. (Luke 15:7 KJV)

"I say to you that likewise there will be more joy in heaven over one sinner who repents than over ninety-nine just persons who need no repentance." (Luke 15:7 NKJV)

20   [through his stripes, I was healed]

But he *was* wounded for our transgressions, *he was* bruised for our iniquities: the chastisement of our peace *was* upon him; and with his stripes we are healed. (Isa. 53:5 KJV)

Who his own self bare our sins in his own body on the tree, that we, being dead to sins, should live unto righteousness: by whose stripes ye were healed. (1 Peter 2:24 KJV)

But He *was* wounded for our transgressions, *He was* bruised for our iniquities; The chastisement for our peace *was* upon Him, And by His stripes we are healed. (Isa. 53:5 NKJV)

who Himself bore our sins in His own body on the tree, that we, having died to sins, might live for righteousness--by whose stripes you were healed. (1 Peter 2:24 NKJV)

21   [Jesus did all the work through his freely giving his life]

Hereby perceive we the love *of God*, because he laid down his life for us: and we ought to lay down *our* lives for the brethren. (1 John 3:16 KJV)

By this we know love, because He laid down His life for us. And we also ought to lay down *our* lives for the brethren. (1 John 3:16 NKJV)

22 [I accepted that his word must be the truth]

But as many as received him, to them gave he power to become the sons of God, *even* to them that believe on his name: Which were born, not of blood, nor of the will of the flesh, nor of the will of man, but of God. And the Word was made flesh, and dwelt among us, (and we beheld his glory, the glory as of the only begotten of the Father,) full of grace and truth. (John 1:12–14 KJV)

In whom ye also *trusted*, after that ye heard the word of truth, the gospel of your salvation: in whom also after that ye believed, ye were sealed with that holy Spirit of promise, (Eph. 1:13 KJV)

But as many as received Him, to them He gave the right to become children of God, to those who believe in His name: who were born, not of blood, nor of the will of the flesh, nor of the will of man, but of God. And the Word became flesh and dwelt among us, and we beheld His glory, the glory as of the only begotten of the Father, full of grace and truth. (John 1:12–14 NKJV)

In Him you also *trusted*, after you heard the word of truth, the gospel of your salvation; in whom also, having believed, you were sealed with the Holy Spirit of promise, (Eph. 1:13 NKJV)

23 [I had turned from the things or pleasures of this world and to God]

Choosing rather to suffer affliction with the people of God, than to enjoy the pleasures of sin for a season; (Heb. 11:25 KJV)

choosing rather to suffer affliction with the people of God than to enjoy the passing pleasures of sin, (Heb. 11:25 NKJV)

24 [his word tells us he will return for us in the twinkling of an eye]

Behold, I shew you a mystery; We shall not all sleep, but we shall all be changed, In a moment, in the twinkling of an eye, at the last trump: for the trumpet shall sound, and the dead shall be raised incorruptible, and we shall be changed. For this corruptible must put on incorruption, and this mortal *must* put on immortality. So when this corruptible shall have put on incorruption, and this mortal shall have put on immortality, then shall be brought to pass the saying that is written, Death is swallowed up in victory. O death , where *is* thy sting? O grave where *is* thy victory? The sting of death *is* sin; and the strength of sin *is* the law. But thanks *be* to God, which giveth us the victory through our Lord Jesus Christ. Therefore, my beloved brethren, be ye stedfast, unmoveable, always abounding in the work of the Lord, forasmuch as ye know that your labour is not in vain in the Lord. (1 Cor. 15:51–58 KJV)

Behold, I tell you a mystery: We shall not all sleep, but we shall all be changed—in a moment, in the twinkling of an eye, at the last trumpet. For the trumpet will sound, and the dead will be raised incorruptible, and we shall be changed. For this corruptible must put on incorruption, and this mortal *must* put on immortality. So when this corruptible has put on incorruption, and this mortal has put on immortality, then shall be brought to pass the saying that is written: "Death is swallowed up in victory. O Death, where *is* your sting? O Hades, where *is* your victory?" The sting of death *is* sin, and the strength of sin *is* the law. But thanks *be* to God, who gives us the victory through our Lord Jesus Christ. Therefore, my beloved brethren, be steadfast, immovable, always abounding in the work of the Lord, knowing that your labor is not in vain in the Lord. (1 Cor. 15:51–58 NKJV)

25 [now is the time and now is the day of salvation]

(For he saith, I have heard thee in a time accepted, and in the day of Salvation have I succoured thee: behold, now *is* the accepted time; behold, now *is* the day of salvation.) (2 Cor. 6:2 KJV)

For He says: "In an acceptable time I have heard you, And in the day of salvation I have helped you." Behold, now *is* the accepted time; behold, now *is* the day of salvation. (2 Cor. 6:2 NKJV)

26 [and forsake not the assembling together of yourself with other fellow Christians]

Let us hold fast the profession of *our* faith without wavering; (for he *is* faithful that promised;) And let us consider one another to provoke unto love and to good works: Not forsaking the assembling of ourselves together, as the manner of some *is*; but exhorting *one another*: and so much the more, as ye see the day approaching. (Heb. 10:23–25 KJV)

Let us hold fast the confession of *our* hope without wavering, for He who promised *is* faithful. And let us consider one another in order to stir up love and good works, not forsaking the assembling of ourselves together, as *is* the manner of some, but exhorting *one another*, and so much the more as you see the Day approaching. (Heb. 10:23–25 NKJV)

<u>27</u>   [I still commit sins of commission and omission and have to ask God's forgiveness]

Therefore to him that knoweth to do good, and doeth *it* not, to him it is sin. (James 4:17 KJV)

Therefore, to him who knows to do good and does not do *it*, to him it is sin. (James 4:17 NKJV)

<u>28</u>   [we have to be careful to listen to that still small voice]

And he said, Go forth, and stand upon the mount before the LORD. And, behold, the LORD passed by, and a great and strong wind rent the mountains, and brake in pieces the rocks before the LORD; *but* the LORD *was* not in the wind: and after the wind an earthquake; *but* the LORD *was* not in the earthquake: And after the earthquake a fire; *but* the LORD *was* not in the fire: and after the fire a still small voice. And it was *so*, when Elijah heard *it*, that he wrapped his face in his mantle, and went out, and stood in the entering in of the cave. And, behold, *there came* a voice unto him, and said, What doest thou here, Elijah? (1 Kings 19:11–13 KJV)

Then He said, "Go out, and stand on the mountain before the LORD." And behold, the LORD passed by, and a great and strong wind tore into the mountains and broke the rocks in pieces before the LORD, *but* the LORD *was* not in the wind; and after the wind an earthquake, *but* the LORD *was* not in the earthquake; and after the earthquake a fire, *but* the LORD *was* not in the fire; and after the fire a still small voice. So it was, when Elijah heard *it*, that he wrapped his face in his mantle and went out and stood in the entrance of the cave. Suddenly a voice *came* to him, and said, "What are you doing here, Elijah?" (1 Kings 19:11–13 NKJV)

29

[The Lord does promise to never leave or forsake us]

(29)

Let your conversation *be* without covetousness; *and be* content with such things as ye have: for he hath said, I will never leave thee, nor forsake thee. So that we may boldly say, the Lord *is* my helper, and I will not fear what man shall do unto me. (Heb. 13:5–6 KJV)

Let *your* conduct *be* without covetousness; *be* content with such things as you have. For He Himself has said, "I will never leave you nor forsake you." So we may boldly say: "The Lord *is* my helper; I will not fear. What can man do to me?" (Heb. 13:5–6 NKJV)

30

[at times it is difficult to understand his ... perfect will in our lives]

I beseech you therefore, brethren, by the mercies of God, that ye present your bodies a living sacrifice, holy, acceptable unto God, *which is* your reasonable service. And be not conformed to this world: but be ye transformed by the renewing of your mind, that ye may prove what *is* that good, and acceptable, and perfect, will of God. (Rom. 12:1–2 KJV)

I beseech you therefore, brethren, by the mercies of God, that you present your bodies a living sacrifice, holy, acceptable to God, *which is* your reasonable service. And do not be conformed to this world, but be transformed by the renewing of your mind, that you may prove what *is* that good and acceptable and perfect will of God. (Rom. 12:1–2 NKJV)

31

[God was going to take care of me]

Therefore I say unto you, Take no thought for your life, what ye shall eat, or what ye shall drink; nor yet for your body, what ye shall put on. Is not the life more than meat,

and the body than raiment? Behold the fowls of the air: for they sow not, neither do they reap, nor gather into barns; yet your heavenly Father feedeth them. Are ye not much better than they? Which of you by taking thought can add one cubit unto his stature? And why take ye thought for raiment? Consider the lilies of the field, how they grow; they toil not, neither do they spin: And yet I say unto you, That even Solomon in all his glory was not arrayed like one of these. Wherefore, if God so clothe the grass of the field, which to day is, and to morrow is cast into the oven, *shall he* not much more *clothe* you, O ye of little faith? Therefore take no thought, saying, What shall we eat? or, What shall we drink? or, Wherewithal shall we be clothed? (For after all these things do the Gentiles seek:) for your heavenly Father knoweth that ye have need of all these things. But seek ye first the kingdom of God, and his righteousness; and all these things shall be added unto you. (Matt. 6:25–33 KJV)

Go to the ant, thou sluggard; consider her ways, and be wise: Which having no guide, overseer, or ruler, Provideth her meat in the summer, *and* gathereth her food in the harvest. (Prov. 6:6–8 KJV)

The steps of a *good* man are ordered by the LORD: and he delighteth in his way. Though he fall, he shall not be utterly cast down: for the LORD upholdeth *him with* his hand. I have been young, and *now* am old; yet have I not seen the righteous forsaken, nor his seed begging bread. (Ps. 37:23–25 KJV)

"Therefore I say to you, do not worry about your life, what you will eat or what you will drink; nor about your body, what you will put on. Is not life more than food and The body more than clothing? Look at the birds of the air, for they neither sow nor reap nor gather into barns; yet your heavenly Father feeds them. Are you not of more value than they? Which of you by worrying can add one cubit to his stature? So why do you worry about clothing? Consider the lilies of the field, how they grow: they neither toil nor spin; and yet I say to you that even Solomon in all his glory was not arrayed like one of these.

Now if God so clothes the grass of the field, which today is, and tomorrow is thrown into the oven, *will He* not much more *clothe* you, O you of little faith? Therefore do not worry, saying, 'What shall we eat?' or 'What shall we drink?' or 'What shall we wear?' For after all these things the Gentiles seek. For your heavenly Father knows that you need all these things. But seek first the kingdom of God and His righteousness, and all these things shall be added to you." (Matt. 6:25–33 NKJV)

Go to the ant, you sluggard! Consider her ways and be wise, Which, having no captain, Overseer or ruler, Provides her supplies in the summer, *And* gathers her food in the harvest. (Prov. 6:6–8 NKJV)

The steps of a *good* man are ordered by the LORD, And He delights in his way. Though he fall, he shall not be utterly cast down; For the LORD upholds *him with* His hand. I have been young, and *now* am old; Yet I have not seen the righteous forsaken, Nor his descendants begging bread. (Ps. 37:23–25 NKJV)

Thank you Lord for your Blessings on me.

(Lyrics by James, Russell and Ed Easter—The Easter Brothers)

As the world looks upon me, as I struggle along,
They say I have nothing, but they are so wrong.
In my heart I'm rejoicing, How I wish they could see.
Thank you Lord for your blessings on me.

There's a roof up above me, I've a good place to sleep,
There's food on my table, and shoes on my feet.
You gave me your love Lord and a fine family,
Thank you Lord for your blessings on me.

Now I know I'm not wealthy and these clothes, they're
not new,
I don't have much money but Lord I have you.
And to me that's all that matters, though the world
cannot see,
Thank you Lord for your blessings on me.

There's a roof up above me, I've a good place to sleep,
There's food on my table, and shoes on my feet.
You gave me your love Lord and a fine family,
Thank you Lord for your blessings on me.

Thank you Lord for your blessings on me.
31

32   [I should tithe]

Will a man rob God? Yet ye have robbed me. But ye say,
Wherein have we robbed thee? In tithes and offerings. Ye
are cursed with a curse: for ye have robbed me, *even* this
whole nation. Bring ye all the tithes into the storehouse,
that there may be meat in mine house, and prove me now
herewith, saith the LORD of hosts, if I will not open you the
windows of heaven, and pour you out a blessing, that *there
shall* not *be room* enough *to receive it.* (Mal. 3:8–10 KJV)

"Will a man rob God? Yet you have robbed Me! But you
say, 'In what way have we robbed You?' In tithes and offerings. You are cursed with a curse, For you have robbed Me,
Even this whole nation. Bring all the tithes into the storehouse, That there may be food in My house, And try Me
now in this," Says the LORD of hosts, "If I will not open
for you the windows of heaven And pour out for you *such*
blessing That *there will* not *be room* enough *to receive it.*
(Mal. 3:8–10 NKJV)

33 [give of the first fruits of my labor]

That thou shalt take of the first of all the fruit of the earth, which thou shalt bring of thy land that the LORD thy God giveth thee, and shalt put *it* in a basket, and shalt go unto the place which the LORD thy God shall choose to place his name there. (Deut. 26:2 KJV)

Tell us therefore, What thinkest thou? Is it lawful to give tribute unto Caesar, or not? But Jesus perceived their wickedness, and said, **Why tempt ye me, *ye* hypocrites? Shew me the tribute money.** And they brought unto him a penny. And he saith unto them, **Whose *is* this image and superscription?** They say unto him, Caesar's. Then saith he unto them, **Render therefore unto Caesar the things which are Caesar's; and unto God the things that are God's.** (Matt. 22:17–21 KJV)

"that you shall take some of the first of all the produce of the ground, which you shall bring from your land that the LORD your God is giving you, and put *it* in a basket and go to the place where the LORD your God chooses to make His name abide." (Deut. 26:2 NKJV)

"Tell us, therefore, what do You think? Is it lawful to pay taxes to Caesar, or not?" But Jesus perceived their wickedness, and said, **"Why do you test Me, *you* hypocrites? Show Me the tax money."** So they brought Him a denarius. And He said to them, **"Whose image and inscription *is* this?"** They said to Him, "Caesar's." And He said to them, **"Render therefore to Caesar the things that are Caesar's, and to God the things that are God's."** (Matt. 22:17–21 NKJV)

34 [He has made my cup run over]

The LORD *is* my shepherd; I shall not want.
He maketh me to lie down in green pastures: he leadeth me beside the still waters.
He restoreth my soul: he leadeth me in the paths of

righteousness for his name's sake.

Yea, though I walk through the valley of the shadow of death, I will fear no evil: for thou *art* with me; thy rod and thy staff they comfort me.

Thou preparest a table before me in the presence of mine enemies: thou anointest my head with oil; my cup runneth over.

Surely goodness and mercy shall follow me all the days of my life: and I will dwell in the house of the LORD for ever. (Ps. 23:1–6 KJV)

Then shall the righteous answer him, saying, Lord, when saw we thee an hungred, and fed *thee*? or thirsty, and gave *thee* drink? When saw we thee a stranger, and took *thee* in? or naked, and clothed *thee*? Or when saw we thee sick, or in prison, and came unto thee? And the King shall answer and say unto them, Verily I say unto you, Inasmuch as ye have done *it* unto one of the least of these my brethren, ye have done *it* unto me. (Matt. 25:37–40 KJV)

The LORD *is* my shepherd; I shall not want.

He makes me to lie down in green pastures; He leads me beside the still waters.

He restores my soul; He leads me in the paths of righteousness For His name's sake.

Yea, though I walk through the valley of the shadow of death, I will fear no evil; For You *are* with me; Your rod and Your staff, they comfort me.

You prepare a table before me in the presence of my enemies; You anoint my head with oil; My cup runs over.

Surely goodness and mercy shall follow me All the days of my life; And I will dwell in the house of the LORD Forever. (Ps. 23:1–6 NKJV)

"Then the righteous will answer Him, saying, 'Lord, when did we see You hungry and feed *You*, or thirsty and give *You* drink? When did we see You a stranger and take *You* in, or naked and clothe *You*? Or when did we see You sick, or in prison, and come to You?' And the King will answer and say to them, 'Assuredly, I say to

you, inasmuch as you did *it* to one of the least of these My brethren, you did *it* to Me.'" (Matt. 25:37–40 NKJV)

35 [I knew there were scriptures warning against strong drink and wine]

Wine *is* a mocker, strong drink *is* raging: and whosoever is deceived thereby is not wise. (Prov. 20:1 KJV)

Wine *is* a mocker, Strong drink *is* a brawler, And whoever is led astray by it is not wise. (Prov. 20:1 NKJV)

36 [Praise through good works and teaching all things which he has commanded us]

Yea, a man may say, Thou hast faith, and I have works: shew me thy faith without thy works, and I will shew thee my faith by my works. (James 2:18 KJV)

And Jesus came and spake unto them, saying, **All power is given unto me in heaven and in earth. Go ye therefore, and teach all nations, baptizing them in the name of the Father, and of the Son, and of the Holy Ghost: Teaching them to observe all things whatsoever I have commanded you: and, lo, I am with you always,** *even* **unto the end of the world.** Amen. (Matt. 28:18–20 KJV)

But someone will say, "You have faith, and I have works." Show me your faith without your works, and I will show you my faith by my works. (James 2:18 NKJV)

And Jesus came and spoke to them, saying, "**All authority has been given to Me in heaven and on earth. Go therefore and make disciples of all the nations, baptizing them in the name of the Father and of the Son and of the Holy Spirit, teaching them to observe all things that I have commanded you; and lo, I am with you always,** *even* **to the end of the age.**" Amen. (Matt. 28:18–20 NKJV)

37   [we are as babes and must start out on the milk of the word]

And I, brethren, could not speak unto you as unto spiritual, but as unto carnal, *even* as unto babes in Christ. I have fed you with milk, and not with meat: for hitherto ye were not able *to bear it*, neither yet now are ye able. For ye are yet carnal: for whereas *there is* among you envying, and strife, and divisions, are ye not carnal, and walk as men? (1 Cor. 3:1–3 KJV)

For when for the time ye ought to be teachers, ye have need that one teach you again which *be* the first principles of the oracles of God; and are become such as have need of milk, and not of strong meat. For every one that useth milk *is* unskilful in the word of righteousness: for he is a babe. But strong meat belongeth to them that are of full age, *even* those who by reason of use have their senses exercised to discern both good and evil. (Heb. 5:12–14 KJV)

And I, brethren, could not speak to you as to spiritual *people* but as to carnal, as to babes in Christ. I fed you with milk and not with solid food; for until now you were not able *to receive it*, and even now you are still not able; for you are still carnal. For where *there are* envy, strife, and divisions among you, are you not carnal and behaving like *mere* men? (1 Cor. 3:1–3 NKJV)

For though by this time you ought to be teachers, you need *someone* to teach you again the first principles of the oracles of God; and you have come to need milk and not solid food. For everyone who partakes *only* of milk *is* unskilled in the word of righteousness, for he is a babe. But solid food belongs to those who are of full age, *that is*, those who by reason of use have their senses exercised to discern both good and evil. (Heb. 5:12–14 NKJV)

38   [Jonas (Jonah) was in the belly of a whale for three days and three nights]

For as Jonas was three days and three nights in the whale's belly; so shall the Son of man be three days and three nights in the heart of the earth. (Matt. 12:40 KJV)

"For as Jonah was three days and three nights in the belly of the great fish, so will the Son of Man be three days and three nights in the heart of the earth." (Matt. 12:40 NKJV)

39   [when she received her glorified body]
(39)

For our conversation is in heaven; from whence also we look for the Saviour, the Lord Jesus Christ: Who shall change our vile body, that it may be fashioned like unto his glorious body, according to the working whereby he is able even to subdue all things unto himself. (Phil. 3:20–21 KJV)

For our citizenship is in heaven, from which we also eagerly wait for the Savior, the Lord Jesus Christ, who will transform our lowly body that it may be conformed to His glorious body, according to the working by which He is able even to subdue all things to Himself. (Phil. 3:20–21 NKJV)

40   [the Lord sent an Angel]

For he shall give his angels charge over thee, to keep thee in all thy ways.
They shall bear thee up in *their* hands, lest thou dash thy foot against a stone. (Ps. 91:11–12 KJV)

For He shall give His angels charge over you, To keep you in all your ways.
In *their* hands they shall bear you up, Lest you dash your foot against a stone. (Ps. 91:11–12 NKJV)

41   [Lord, I can do this with your help]

I can do all things through Christ which strengtheneth me. (Phil. 4:13 KJV)

I can do all things through Christ who strengthens me. (Phil. 4:13 NKJV)

42   [he must have been born again]

There was a man of the Pharisees, named Nicodemus, a ruler of the Jews: The same came to Jesus by night, and said unto him, Rabbi, we know that thou art a teacher come from God: for no man can do these miracles that thou doest, except God be with him. Jesus answered and said unto him, **Verily, verily, I say unto thee, Except a man be born again, he cannot see the kingdom of God.** Nicodemus saith unto him, How can a man be born when he is old? can he enter the second time into his mother's womb, and be born? Jesus answered, **Verily, verily, I say unto thee, Except a man be born of water and *of* the Spirit, he cannot enter into the kingdom of God. That which is born of the flesh is flesh; and that which is born of the Spirit is spirit. Marvel not that I said unto thee, Ye must be born again. The wind bloweth where it listeth, and thou hearest the sound thereof, but canst not tell whence it cometh, and whither it goeth: so is every one that is born of the Spirit.** (John 3:1–8 KJV)

There was a man of the Pharisees named Nicodemus, a ruler of the Jews. This man came to Jesus by night and said to Him, "Rabbi, we know that You are a teacher come from God; for no one can do these signs that You do unless God is with him." Jesus answered and said to him, **"Most assuredly, I say to you, unless one is born again, he cannot see the kingdom of God."** Nicodemus said to Him, "How can a man be born when he is old? Can he enter a second time into his mother's womb and be born?" Jesus answered, **"Most assuredly, I say to you, unless one is born of water and the Spirit, he cannot enter the kingdom of God.**

That which is born of the flesh is flesh, and that which is born of the Spirit is spirit. Do not marvel that I said to you, 'You must be born again.' The wind blows where it wishes, and you hear the sound of it, but cannot tell where it comes from and where it goes. So is everyone who is born of the Spirit. " (John 3:1–8 NKJV)

43   [I might have gone on to be in his presence]

For we know that if our earthly house of *this* tabernacle were dissolved, we have a building of God, an house not made with hands, eternal in the heavens. For in this we groan, earnestly desiring to be clothed upon with our house which is from heaven: If so be that being clothed we shall not be found naked. For we that are in *this* tabernacle do groan, being burdened: not for that we would be unclothed, but clothed upon, that mortality might be swallowed up of life. Now he that hath wrought us for the selfsame thing *is* God, who also hath given unto us the earnest of the Spirit. Therefore *we are* always confident, knowing that, whilst we are at home in the body, we are absent from the Lord: (For we walk by faith, not by sight:) We are confident, *I say*, and willing rather to be absent from the body, and to be present with the Lord. Wherefore we labour, that, whether present or absent, we may be accepted of him. For we must all appear before the judgment seat of Christ; that every one may receive the things *done* in *his* body, according to that he hath done, whether *it be* good or bad. (2 Cor. 5:1–10 KJV)

For we know that if our earthly house, *this* tent, is destroyed, we have a building from God, a house not made with hands, eternal in the heavens. For in this we groan, earnestly desiring to be clothed with our habitation which is from heaven, if indeed, having been clothed, we shall not be found naked. For we who are in *this* tent groan, being burdened, not because we want to be unclothed, but further clothed, that mortality may be swallowed up by life. Now He who has prepared us for this very thing *is* God, who also has given us the Spirit as a guarantee. So *we are* always confident, knowing that while we are at home in the body we are absent from the Lord. For we walk by faith, not by sight. We are confident, yes, well pleased rather to be absent from the body and to be present with the Lord. Therefore we make it our aim, whether present or absent, to be well pleasing to Him. For we must all appear before the judgment seat of Christ, that each one may receive the things *done* in the body, according to what he has done, whether good or bad. (2 Cor. 5:1–10 NKJV)

44 [I have always believed strongly that all things will work out to the good]

And we know that all things work together for good to them that love God, to them who are the called according to *his* purpose. (Rom. 8:28 KJV)

And we know that all things work together for good to those who love God, to those who are the called according to *His* purpose. (Rom. 8:28 NKJV)

45 [rightly divided his word of truth]

Study to shew thyself approved unto God, a workman that needeth not to be ashamed, rightly dividing the word of truth. (2 Tim. 2:15 KJV)

Be diligent to present yourself approved to God, a worker who does not need to be ashamed, rightly dividing the word of truth. (2 Tim. 2:15 NKJV)

46 [It has always been my desire...]

Wherefore seeing we also are compassed about with so great a cloud of witnesses, let us lay aside every weight, and the sin which doth so easily beset *us*, and let us run with patience the race that is set before us, Looking unto Jesus the author and finisher of *our* faith; who for the joy that was set before him endured the cross, despising the shame, and is set down at the right hand of the throne of God. (Heb. 12:1–2 KJV)

His lord said unto him, Well done, *thou* good and faithful servant: thou hast been faithful over a few things, I will make thee ruler over many things: enter thou into the joy of thy lord. (Matt. 25:21 KJV)

Wherefore we labour, that, whether present or absent, we may be accepted of him. For we must all appear before the judgment seat of Christ; that every one may receive the things *done* in *his* body, according to that he hath done, whether *it be* good or bad. (2 Cor. 5:9–10 KJV)

Therefore we also, since we are surrounded by so great a cloud of witnesses, let us lay aside every weight, and the sin which so easily ensnares *us*, and let us run with endurance the race that is set before us, looking unto Jesus, the author and finisher of *our* faith, who for the joy that was set before Him endured the cross, despising the shame, and has sat down at the right hand of the throne of God. (Heb. 12:1–2 NKJV)

"His lord said to him, 'Well *done*, good and faithful servant; you were faithful over a few things, I will make you ruler over many things. Enter into the joy of your lord.'" (Matt. 25:21 NKJV)

Therefore we make it our aim, whether present or absent, to be well pleasing to Him. For we must all appear before the judgment seat of Christ, that each one may receive the things *done* in the body, according to what he has done, whether good or bad. (2 Cor. 5:9–10 NKJV)

About the Author

Born; August 13, 1947 - New Orleans, LA

Born Again; October 17, 1976 - Gastonia, NC
John Chapter 3: 1 - 7

Present with the Lord; To Be Announced
2 Corinthians 5: 6-10

CPSIA information can be obtained at www.ICGtesting.com
Printed in the USA
BVOW040454030512

289182BV00001B/2/P